Contents

Words in **CAPITALS** are further explained in the glossary on page 48.

▲ These historical dolls show King Henry VIII and his six wives.

You can easily remember what happened to each of Henry VIII's wives by learning this rhyme. Just read from top to bottom. The colours match the contents list:

Divorced

Beheaded

Died

Divorced

Beheaded

Survived

The start of Tudor times

The Tudor kings and queens wanted to keep their power – this was usually achieved through marriage.

The first of the **TUDOR** kings and queens (monarchs) was Henry VII, also known as Henry Tudor. He became king in 1485, when he and his troops won the Battle of Bosworth. His reign began one of the most famous periods of English history, but far more famous was his younger son, who became Henry VIII.

Henry VIII's life is famous. But what of his wives? In this book, we shall look at the times of Henry VIII from the point of view of each wife, and try to work out what they thought of the husband they had in common – Henry.

The Tudors and Europe

Henry VIII had to rule England *and* keep an eye on what was happening in Europe.

▲ ① The Tudor Rose.

Survival often depended on having support from other countries, and in Tudor times this was achieved by marriages between the royal households.

▼ ② The House of Tudor. You can see why Henry VIII was so keen to have male heirs. Without heirs the kings of Scotland, France and Spain could claim the English throne.

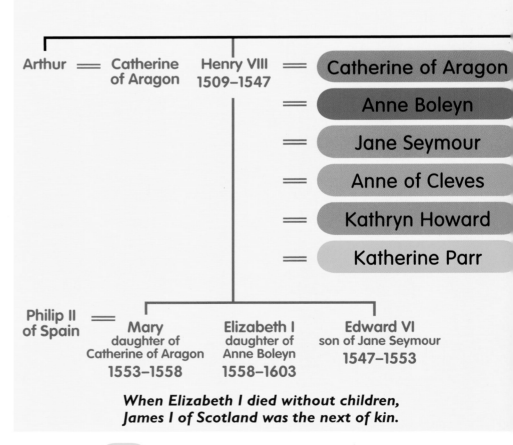

Tudor claim to the throne

Arthur ═ Catherine of Aragon ═ Henry VIII 1509–1547 ═ Catherine of Aragon

═ Anne Boleyn

═ Jane Seymour

═ Anne of Cleves

═ Kathryn Howard

═ Katherine Parr

Philip II of Spain ═ Mary daughter of Catherine of Aragon 1553–1558

Elizabeth I daughter of Anne Boleyn 1558–1603

Edward VI son of Jane Seymour 1547–1553

When Elizabeth I died without children, James I of Scotland was the next of kin.

Henry Tudor (Henry VII)

The royal Tudor line began with Henry Tudor (1457–1509) (picture ②). He was the first Tudor king.

Henry VII had to try to rebuild a country whose **NOBLE** families had been warring for many years. This **CIVIL WAR** was called the Wars of the Roses. The wars were called the Wars of the Roses because one side supported the nobles from York (whose symbol was a white rose) and the other side supported the nobles from Lancaster (whose symbol was a red rose).

Henry Tudor was related to the House of Lancaster. By marrying Elizabeth of York the Yorkists and the Lancastrians were brought together. The Tudors adopted as their symbol a white rose inside a red rose, symbolising the joining of the two houses (picture ①).

You can already start to see how things worked. So much was at stake, that marriages were planned for the good of the country. When it worked, it worked well.

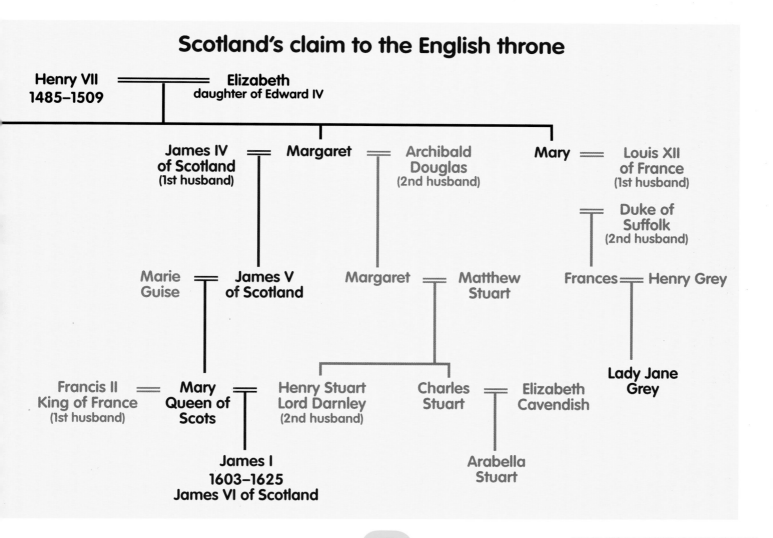

Scotland's claim to the English throne

Henry VII 1485–1509 ══ Elizabeth daughter of Edward IV

James IV of Scotland (1st husband) ══ Margaret ══ Archibald Douglas (2nd husband)   Mary ══ Louis XII of France (1st husband)

══ Duke of Suffolk (2nd husband)

Marie Guise ══ James V of Scotland   Margaret ══ Matthew Stuart   Frances ══ Henry Grey

Francis II King of France (1st husband) ══ Mary Queen of Scots ══ Henry Stuart Lord Darnley (2nd husband)   Charles Stuart ══ Elizabeth Cavendish   Lady Jane Grey

James I 1603–1625 James VI of Scotland

Arabella Stuart

Henry VIII

Henry knew his word was absolute law, and he behaved like it.

How should we think about Henry VIII as a man and as a husband? In modern language we would call Henry a 'control freak'. For example, Henry VIII was the first English king to insist on being called "Your Majesty".

The young Henry

We're used to seeing paintings of Henry VIII looking fat and, perhaps, a bit tired (picture ① inset and page 1). When he died, he measured 54 inches around the waist! But when he was young there had also been a charming, handsome, 6ft 2in (1.88m) and sporting Henry (picture ①) who came to the throne at the age of 18.

Henry liked to live well, but this needed money. Henry would almost be called a 'spendaholic' today.

He certainly spent more money than he could afford. He could not raise taxes to pay for his spending, so he had to look for other ways to get money. One common way was to marry a wife who brought a large **DOWRY** with her. This was probably the reason he married more than one of his wives.

His advisors were quick to point out that the Roman Catholic church was much wealthier than the king.

As we shall see, Henry was able to change all that.

Many women

Young Henry put all of his enormous energy into sport, music and many other interests. He loved to paint and took a keen interest in education.

Henry also fell in love easily, and moved his love from one woman to another. He was not faithful and had a large number of **MISTRESSES** besides the wives we shall be reading about.

Henry had a fierce temper. When enraged, the king became "the most dangerous and cruel man in the world." This was the side his earlier wives found out about – to their cost.

The elderly Henry

As he grew older, the king became suspicious of everyone and he could easily turn on old friends and even have them executed. This made life in court very dangerous.

This was the Henry his later wives grew to know (and often to hate).

▶ ① Henry VIII as a young man and, inset, as an older man.

A matter of uniform

In Tudor England, class was very important. In previous times the people with power were the lords of the land, but this was changing. Now merchants were growing in wealth and influence. Henry brought in strict laws so that he could tell at a glance whether he was looking at a noble or a wealthy merchant. He did this by controlling what they could wear. Velvet and satin could only be worn by men above the rank of knight. Gold, silver or purple cloth could only be worn by women with the rank of countess or higher. No woman was allowed to wear cloth embroidered with silk, pearls, gold or silver except baronesses and above.

Kings, Pope and the Protestants

What a complicated world it was! Everyone in power was trying to win control of Europe.

Kings were not the only powerful people in Tudor times. All European countries were **CATHOLIC** and the head of the Catholic Church was the Pope.

The Pope

The Pope was just as political as anyone else, and he had lots of ways of getting kings to do what he wanted. He could, if he wished, expel a king from the church (called excommunication) and tell them they would not go to heaven when they died. Most kings were afraid of this.

The Protestants

As it happened, many people in Europe were not pleased to be ruled by the Pope. These people were called **REFORMERS** or Protestants, because they wanted to change, or *reform*, the church and they protested about Catholic rules. For our story, we should note that at this time there were people in Europe setting up an alternative religion to Catholicism.

The king

As our story unfolds, we find Henry Tudor (Henry VII) has died and Henry VIII has taken over as king. Henry is a devout Catholic and he is bitterly opposed to the Reformers and in favour of the Pope. However that will change as we shall see.

The king's advisors

The king had two important advisors, Archbishop Thomas Cranmer (picture ①) and Thomas Cromwell. They, like many other people, wanted more power and so they began to convince the king that he, and not the Pope, should head the church in England. They also pointed out that the Pope's church in England was very, very wealthy. Henry was already spending more of the royal money than he should. So, if the king could become head of the church in England, he could go on spending as much money as he wanted (picture ②).

These arguments appealed to the young king when he wanted to do something the Pope would not allow… as we shall see.

The wives

So now you know a little about Henry and early Tudor times. This is the world into which his wives got entangled. So let us look at the story of each of the wives and see how they got on with this handsome but cruel man.

► ① **Thomas Cranmer, Archbishop of Canterbury.**

► ② **This important historic parchment is the statement signed by Thomas Cranmer and seven other English bishops, declaring the authority of the king over church matters in England. It is the founding document of the Church of England.**

Catherine of Aragon

The first wife whose marriage also lasted the longest.

Catherine of Aragon was the youngest child of King Ferdinand and Queen Isabella of Spain. Spain was the most important country in Europe.

As was common for princesses of the day, as soon as she was born her parents began looking for someone to marry her to.

When she was three years old, the match was made to Arthur, the eldest son of Henry Tudor (Henry VII) of England. Arthur was not even two years old at the time!

Catherine of Aragon

Born:	1485
Married:	11ᵗˢ June 1509
Divorced/ annulled:	1533
Married for:	24 years
Died:	7ᵗˢ January 1536 (aged 50)
Life after divorce:	3 years

◄ ① Prince Arthur.

Arthur's wife

In 1501, when she was almost 16, Catherine came to England. After the wedding, Arthur and Catherine lived at Ludlow Castle. But, six months later, Arthur (picture ①) became ill and died.

Catherine remarries

Catherine (picture ②) was now a widow, but still young enough to be married again. Her father-in-law, Henry VII, still wanted Catherine's **DOWRY**, which had not yet been paid in full. So, 14 months after her husband's death, Catherine was promised to the future Henry VIII, who was still too young to marry.

Unfortunately, by 1505, when Henry was old enough to get married, his father no longer wanted an alliance with Spain, so the marriage was cancelled. Then, in 1509, Henry Tudor died and his son Henry became King Henry VIII.

One of the first things Henry did was to marry Catherine (because he wanted the dowry!). As a result, Spanish Catherine was crowned Queen of England on 24 June, 1509.

Children

Henry and Catherine had a son, Prince Henry, who was born on

▲ ② Catherine of Aragon was a faithful wife even though Henry had many mistresses.

1 January, 1511. This was just what the king wanted – an heir. Sadly, the baby died 52 days later. Henry and Catherine tried again. Catherine then had a MISCARRIAGE, followed by a second son who also died shortly after birth. Then, in February 1516, she had a daughter named Mary (later to become Queen Mary) (picture ③).

When Catherine reached 42 she was getting beyond child-bearing age, and so Henry no longer wanted to stay married to her. During this time King Henry fell in love with many attractive women at court, including one of Catherine's ladies-in-waiting (and the sister of one of his other mistresses): Anne Boleyn (see pages 16 to 21).

Henry and Anne Boleyn

It did not take the court long to begin to whisper about Anne Boleyn and the king. Henry still wanted a male heir, so he sent representatives to ask the Pope to end the marriage so he could marry Anne Boleyn.

◄ ③ Catherine's daughter, Mary, who became Queen Mary.

The Pope says no

When Catherine found out about Henry's plans, she asked the Pope to refuse the request. The Pope suggested to Catherine that she might enter a CONVENT. This would automatically cancel her marriage, but she refused because that would mean that her daughter, Mary, would have lost her right to the throne of England.

Catherine is forced out

Things came to a head in 1533 when Henry caused Anne Boleyn to become PREGNANT. But still the Pope would not give a divorce as this was against Catholic law.

This is when Henry's advisors told him to break with the Catholic Church and become a Protestant, and at the same time become head of the Church in England and so gain the wealth of the church. When Henry did this, the Pope excommunicated him. Henry's court then forced Catherine to give up being queen and leave court. She lived the rest of her life in various castles. She died at Kimbolton Castle in 1536 aged 50.

Catherine's story

My marriage to Arthur was decided when I was just three years old. This was the normal way of doing things and I grew up knowing that my fate was to one day become Queen of England. Of course, things did not end up the way I thought they would.

My parents were the most famous royal people in all of Europe. I was lucky, because this meant that, unlike most women, I was taught to read and write Latin and French and other subjects as well as the traditional wife's skills – embroidery, music, dance, drawing and cooking. As a Catholic, I was taught not only that God blessed a king's reign, but that any marriage between king and queen was God's will.

I went to England when I was 15 and Arthur and I were married in a grand ceremony. Just a few months later we both became very ill and Arthur died. I was very ill for a long time and when I recovered, the King of England and my parents decided that I should marry Arthur's brother, Henry. I did not know Henry very well, but I was very happy that I had a future. Henry was very tall and handsome and he loved hunting and other sports.

During Henry's first years as king, I often advised him and helped to run the country, but soon Cardinal Wolsey began to have the king's ear more and more, and I was given less and less to do with the affairs of state.

I looked forward to having a son who would grow up to be King of England, but it was not to be. I had many pregnancies, but only one child who lived. Doctors said that the miscarriages might have been caused by my long illness.

continued...

Many years went by and I know that Henry was seeing other women, but I kept quiet as a dignified queen should. Then Henry became very unhappy and asked me for a divorce, but as a good Catholic, I do not believe in divorce. Then he asked the Pope to convince me to join a convent. That way, I would be married to God and my marriage to Henry could be cancelled. But if I did that, Mary, my daughter, would never be queen. When I found out that Henry had asked the Pope for the marriage to be cancelled, I knew I had to act.

Luckily, the Pope is good friends with my nephew, King Charles I of Spain, so the Pope took my side and refused to cancel the marriage. But Henry was listening to Wolsey and to his Archbishop, Thomas Cranmer. They were greedy for power. Cranmer convinced Henry that he, and not the Pope, should be head of the Church in England. That way, he could make any religious rules he liked. Cranmer declared that our marriage was against God's law, because I had been married to Henry's brother, Arthur, first.

I was told that I had no choice but to accept the divorce and let Henry marry Anne Boleyn. But I refused – I did not believe in divorce and I would not give up Mary's claim to the throne. Even though Henry had already married Anne Boleyn, I refused to give her my crown jewels. I told Henry that his new wife was the scandal of Christendom and a disgrace to him. Because I refused to co-operate, Henry made Mary and me live in one draughty old castle after another.

I always refused to let anyone use my new title "Dowager Princess of Wales" and ignored anyone who did not address me as queen. From time to time, the king sent royal envoys to have me swear the oath that recognised Henry's marriage to Anne Boleyn as lawful. I always told them, "I am queen and queen I will die."

In her own words:

Even under fire, Catherine of Aragon never became flustered. She was well known for keeping to her principles and she made a powerful speech during the 1529 hearing into her marriage to Henry VIII. This is what she said:

"Sir, I beseech you for all the love that hath been between us, let me have justice and right, take of me some pity and compassion, for I am a poor woman, and a stranger, born out of your dominion. I have here no friend and much less indifferent counsel. I flee to you, as to the head of justice within this realm . . . I take God and all the world to witness that I have been to you a true, humble and obedient wife, ever comfortable to your will and pleasure . . . being always well pleased and contented with all things wherein you had any delight or dalliance . . .

I loved all those whom ye loved, only for your sake, whether I had cause or no, and whether they were my friends or enemies. This 20 years or more I have been your true wife and by me ye have had divers children, although it hath pleased God to call them from this world, which hath been no default in me. . .

And when ye had me at first, I take God to my judge, I was a true maid, without touch of man. And whether this be true or no, I put it to your conscience . . . Therefore, I humbly require you to spare me the extremity of this new court . . .

And if ye will not, to God I commit my cause."

Catherine of Aragon

Anne Boleyn

Scheming Anne was the first mistress turned queen to lose her head.

Little is known about Anne's early years. She was probably born in 1500 or 1501.

What was Anne like?

Anne (picture ①) was witty, confident, and full of herself – not quiet, gentle or timid (which is what a 16th century woman was supposed to be like). She was charming and talkative, but also had a fiery temper which she never learned to control.

The early years

Anne learned to play many musical instruments, to sing and to dance. When she was 12, Anne's father managed to get her into the Belgian court. Two years later, she moved to the court of Henry VIII's sister, Mary, who was, by now, the Queen of France.

Anne meets Henry

Around 1521 Anne went to the English court to attend Queen Catherine as maid-of-honour.

Exactly when and where Henry VIII first noticed Anne, no-one quite knows. But King Henry VIII's devotion to Anne caused him to write love letters to her when she was away from court, even though Henry hated writing letters.

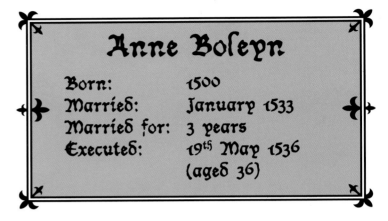

Anne Boleyn

Born: 1500
Married: January 1533
Married for: 3 years
Executed: 19th May 1536
                  (aged 36)

Anne and Catherine

By 1528, Anne had become well known at court. Everyone also soon knew of her relationship with the king.

It was at this time that Henry wanted to divorce Catherine, but it all took a long time, and this did not suit fiery-tempered Anne. As a result, she had famous arguments with Henry right in front of the courtiers. Anne was worried that Henry might decide to stay with Catherine if the divorce did not happen quickly and she would have wasted time that she could have used to make another profitable marriage.

Unpopular Anne

The people of England liked Catherine and were not pleased to see Anne living with the king while Catherine was still queen.

◄ ① Anne Boleyn, first Henry's mistress, and then the second of his wives.

▶ ② Anne's daughter, Princess Elizabeth, age 14, who became Queen Elizabeth I.

Of course, it was in Anne's interests to have Henry leave the Catholic Church, as then he would get his divorce. So she supported the Reformers in England, but this was not popular with many people in England either.

Because Anne was scheming to get power, she made many enemies at court. She schemed to try to have Cardinal Wolsey banished from court. He was, of course, too clever to let that happen and then he waited to get his revenge.

Anne led fashion

The fashion leaders in Europe were the French, and as Anne had been at the French court it was easy for her to know about French fashion and get the latest French fashions made. Everyone else at court might have hated Anne, but they needed to be fashionable so they copied these styles, just as we follow the styles of famous people today.

Anne as queen

By December 1532 Henry had made Anne pregnant even though they were not married.

Sometime around 25 January, 1533, Anne and Henry were secretly married. Then, on 23 May, the Archbishop officially proclaimed that the marriage of Henry and Catherine was invalid.

On 1 June, 1533, Anne was crowned queen and, on 7 September, 1533, Elizabeth (later Queen Elizabeth I) was born (picture ②).

Treason

As you know, the king easily fell in and out of love. Now he was losing interest in Anne because he had found a new lover – Jane Seymour – Anne's maid-of-honour.

This was just what Anne's enemies at court were waiting for. The king's chief advisor, Thomas Cromwell, began to plot to bring down the queen. On 30 April, 1536, Anne's friend Mark Smeaton, was arrested and tortured into confessing that he and Anne had commited **ADULTERY**.

On 2 May, the queen was arrested on charges of **TREASON**. She was then taken to the Tower, quickly found guilty and sentenced to death. Shortly before her execution, the queen's marriage to the king was set aside.

Anne was beheaded on 19 May.

Anne's story

My life began in a very normal way for a lady of noble birth. When I was 12 years old, I was sent to be a lady-in-waiting at the court of the Archduchess Margaret. Being a lady-in-waiting is how high-born girls are taught how to behave at court. As a lady-in-waiting I had a chance to learn all about art, music, dance, conversation and how to be the wife of a nobleman. It was expected that I would marry a nobleman.

After a few years with Margaret, I was transferred to the household of Mary Tudor, who was married to Louis XII, King of France. I loved France and soon learned to speak and read French and to love French art, music and clothes. When I was 20, I was told to return to England, to wait on Queen Catherine, because my parents were arranging for my marriage to the son of the Duke of Ormonde.

The plans for my marriage fell through and I began looking around for another rich nobleman to marry. But living at court, I soon attracted the attention of the king. I decided immediately that I would like to be queen, but I had to be careful, Henry was still married, and he had a lot of other mistresses, but he promised that as soon as his marriage to Catherine was cancelled by the Pope, he would marry me. The years dragged on, I became tired of waiting for the divorce. Every time I got angry at waiting, Henry would buy me more jewellery and clothes as gifts to make me feel better, but after more than six years of waiting, I became pregnant and Henry decided he had to marry me. Of course, the ceremony had to be kept secret.

continued...

After the divorce to Catherine finally happened, I was crowned on 1 June, 1533, at Westminster Abbey. As we rode in a magnificent procession from the Tower of London to Westminster, Londoners cried "HA! HA!" as a joke on our initials – Henry and Anne. It seems that the people loved Catherine of Aragon and hated me.

Although Henry was pleased to have a child, I know he was disappointed it wasn't a boy. I was disappointed as well. I knew only too well that I had many enemies at court and the only way to remain queen was to give Henry a son, but after two more miscarriages, Henry grew tired of waiting for a boy. He began to see my maid-of-honour Jane Seymour, and my enemies decided to act against me.

I had made many enemies at court because of my support for the Reformers. My worst enemy was Thomas Cromwell, who had always resented my influence over the king.

My maids were pressured, under pain of torture I have no doubt, into telling stories about me having men to my bed chamber at late hours and I was charged with conspiracy to murder the king and adultery with four men: my favourite musician, Mark Smeaton, and other men were also charged. But the worst was the charge of making love to my own brother, George. This was simply untrue, but his wife was jealous of me so she gave false evidence against us.

I was tried on made up charges of adultery. They were all lies, but it didn't matter, adultery by the queen is treason, and in a treason trial there can be no defence. I am only sorry that so many innocent men had to die with me. Of course, they would not have been charged if they, too, had not also made many enemies at court. That is how life is at court. One day you are the king's favourite, the next day your enemies have won and you have lost your head.

In her own words:

Anne Boleyn's speech at her execution, 19 May, 1536, at 8:00am:

Good Christian people, I am come hither to die, for according to the law, and by the law I am judged to die, and therefore I will speak nothing against it. I am come hither to accuse no man, nor to speak anything of that, whereof I am accused and condemned to die, but I pray God save the king and send him long to reign over you, for a gentler nor a more merciful prince was there never: and to me he was ever a good, a gentle and sovereign lord. And if any person will meddle of my cause, I require them to judge the best. And thus I take my leave of the world and of you all, and I heartily desire you all to pray for me. O Lord have mercy on me, to God I commend my soul.

Anne Boleyn

After being blindfolded and kneeling at the block, she repeated several times:

"To Jesus Christ I commend my soul; Lord Jesu receive my soul."

Jane Seymour

Young Jane Seymour was Henry's favourite wife, but she soon died.

Jane Seymour first came to court to wait on Queen Catherine, but was then moved to become Anne Boleyn's maid-of-honour. This is where King Henry first noticed Jane. It was said that Jane's sweet and charming demeanour captured Henry's heart. Married just days after Anne Boleyn's death, she was to become Henry's favourite wife.

What was Jane like?

Jane Seymour could not have been more different to Anne (picture ①). She was what a 16th century woman should be… silent, timid and sweet-tempered.

Jane was not highly educated. In fact, she could only read and write her name. She was not witty like Anne Boleyn, nor intelligent like Catherine of Aragon.

She received the education typical for women of her time: needlework and household management. But Jane was more clever than others might have thought. After waiting on Catherine of Aragon and Anne Boleyn, Jane had learned the cut-throat ways of Henry VIII's court. And she had learned those lessons well.

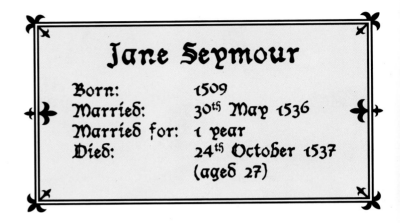

Jane Seymour

Born: 1509
Married: 30ᵗʰ May 1536
Married for: 1 year
Died: 24ᵗʰ October 1537
(aged 27)

Henry's lover

Jane was Henry's third wife, and she could have been in no doubt that having Henry for a lover was a dangerous thing.

Of course, once the king had chosen her as a mistress there was absolutely nothing she could do about it anyway. But being able to fit in with Henry's changeable moods was no doubt very helpful. There were no public arguments as there had been with Anne.

Jane had to worry not just for herself, but also for her family. If she fell out of favour with the king, her family could suffer, too, as Henry would take his revenge.

On the other hand, being a mistress often meant that the king gave riches and titles to the whole family.

► ① Jane Seymour would probably have remained Henry's wife, if she had lived.

23

When he was courting Jane, Henry gave her a present of gold coins. Jane refused the money and begged the king to remember that she was an honourable woman. She said she would "rather die a thousand times" than tarnish her honour. Henry was impressed with her modesty and made up his mind to marry her.

Queen Jane

Just a day after Anne Boleyn's execution, Jane Seymour and Henry VIII agreed to marry and on 30 May, the ceremony took place.

Henry often referred to Jane as his 'first real wife', and he was probably grateful for a more quiet life than he had had up to that time.

Queen Jane never had a coronation. The coronation was put off, first because Henry was short of money to pay for it, and then because of trouble in the North of England that needed Henry's attention. In the end, Jane died before it could be held.

Jane became pregnant in early 1537. Prince Edward was born in October. This was the male heir Henry wanted (picture ③, page 26).

The birth had been difficult and had greatly weakened Jane. She died on 24 October, just two weeks after her son was born (picture ②). Henry was very upset by Jane's death and for a time he refused to see anyone.

Henry's fond memories

In his later years, Henry would remember his time with Jane as the happiest in his life. In 1543, during Henry's marriage to Katherine Parr, he commissioned a painting with his three children and his wife. But instead of Queen Katherine at his side, it was Jane Seymour. When Henry died in 1547, he left instructions to be buried with this most beloved of all his wives.

▼ ② **Westminster Abbey, Jane Seymour's burial place.**

Jane's story

My parents always taught me that a proper lady should be silent, obedient and sweet-tempered. They did not approve of education for women and so I did not learn to read and write more than my name. Instead, I was taught wifely skills of household management and needlework. But when I was at court, as maid-of-honour to Queen Catherine and to Anne Boleyn, I also learned the ways of getting along at court.

I had been at court for six years as maid-of-honour to Catherine of Aragon and Anne Boleyn when the king began to pay attention to me. As he was still married, I refused to make love to him, but this only made him want me more. When it became obvious that the king was interested in me, those who were against Anne Boleyn, and especially those who were still Catholics, rushed to my side to help me.

Because I am a good Catholic and do not approve of the Reformation, they hoped that I would encourage the king to return to the 'true faith' and give up Reform.

After we were married, I helped Henry and his elder daughter, Mary, to get together again. Mary was a good Catholic, like me, and my hope was that Mary could eventually become queen and end the Reformation. When rebellions broke out in 1536, and the people demanded the restoration of the Catholic Church, I tried to convince the king to listen, but Henry exploded with anger and reminded me of what had happened to his other queens, so I learned my place and did not interfere in the affairs of state.

After I became pregnant, the king made sure I had everything I could want. Once I had a craving for quails, and so Henry had some shipped all the way from Calais in France.

continued...

On 12 October, 1537, I gave birth to a son – Edward. I had been in labour for three days. Although I felt good, if a bit weak, after the birth, I soon took ill with a fever, which was very common. When the end came for me, I had been queen for just 18 months, but I had fulfilled the greatest task of a Tudor queen, I had given the king a male heir.

◀ ③ Prince Edward (later Edward VI).

In her own words:

Letter of Queen Jane Seymour to the **PRIVY COUNCIL** of England
12 October, 1537:

(Upon the birth of Prince Edward, this letter was immediately sent to the
Privy Council to announce the arrival of Henry VIII's long awaited heir.
Though Queen Jane is not thought to have written the letter herself, it was
sent in her name and had her seal. It was probably dictated to a secretary.)

Right trusty and well beloved, we greet you well, and
for as much as by the inestimable goodness and grace of
Almighty God, we be delivered and brought in childbed of
a prince, conceived in most lawful matrimony between my
lord the king's majesty and us, doubting not but that for
the love and affection which you bear unto us and to the
commonwealth of this realm, the knowledge thereof should
be joyous and glad tidings unto you, we have thought
good to certify you of the same. To the intent you might
not only render unto God condign thanks and prayers for
so great a benefit but also continually pray for the long
continuance and preservation of the same here in this life
to the honour of God, joy and pleasure of my lord the king
and us, and the universal weal, quiet and tranquillity
of this whole realm. Given under our signet at
my lord's manor of Hampton Court the 12th
day of October.

Jane the Queen

Anne of Cleves

Poor, plain Anne – or so Henry thought – lasted less than a year. But she thought him ugly, too.

The shock Henry felt at Jane Seymour's death was real, but that was not the reason he stayed unmarried for over two years. In fact, one of Henry's advisors, Thomas Cromwell, began looking for another wife shortly after Jane's death. Politics was rearing its ugly head again.

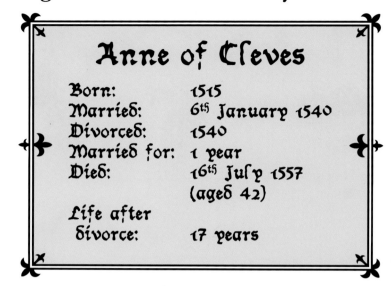

Anne of Cleves

Born:	1515
Married:	6th January 1540
Divorced:	1540
Married for:	1 year
Died:	16th July 1557 (aged 42)
Life after divorce:	17 years

What could be gained?

Henry's first marriage was brought about for political reasons. Both Spain and England wanted to gain by it. But Henry's next two wives had not been useful to England in Europe, for he married people from England.

Henry was quite clear about why he needed a fourth wife, whether she came from England or Europe: more sons. In an age when many children died young, he needed more than Prince Edward to help make sure the Tudor line continued.

Henry is weak

After Henry broke from the Pope he did not have many allies left in Europe, because most countries were still Catholic. But Henry didn't want to get himself stuck with an ugly woman either, so he had agents in foreign courts report to him on the appearance and other qualities of various candidates. He also sent painters to bring him images of these women.

Hans Holbein, a famous court painter, was sent to the court of the Duke of Cleves (now part of Germany), to paint his two sisters, Amelia and Anne, and send the portraits back for Henry to see.

Holbein painted them as flatteringly as he normally would for any noble, although this turned out to be a disaster.

When Henry saw the painting he thought that Anne was very attractive, and ordered the marriage arrangements to begin (picture ①).

Anne, of course, had little to say about this, but it was always going to be difficult as she had never been away from the German court, she

◀ ① Anne of Cleves.

had not been brought up with music or the knowledge of fine books that everyone had in the English court. She spoke no English and knew nothing about England. She may even not have known where it was.

The 'Flanders mare'

When Henry first met her, just before the wedding, he realised that he had fallen into a ghastly mistake. In his eyes she was unattractive, and "gave off evil smells". Since most people at this time only washed every few months, if that, the probable reason Henry thought she smelled was that she was not in the habit of disguising the smell of her body with perfume. Henry called her the 'Flanders mare'. As it happened, Anne was very humble, and this is probably what saved her.

The marriage took place on 6 January, 1540, although by then, Henry was already looking for ways to get out of it. Not only did Henry not like Anne (she did not like him either), but Cleves was being drawn into a war that Henry wanted no part of, and last, but not least, Henry had become attracted to young, pretty Kathryn Howard.

Paid off

Anne was probably clever enough to know that she would only make trouble for herself if she started to object to having the marriage set aside. She even said in public that they had not made love and that her previous engagement (at the age of 12) to the son of the Duke of Lorraine had not been properly broken.

This all worked in Anne's favour. Anne accepted the honorary title of 'King's Sister', and did very well financially. She was given property, including Hever Castle (picture ②), once the home of Anne Boleyn. Now that she had money of her own and was not likely to lose her head, Anne was able to enjoy herself better. Funnily enough, she also stayed on speaking terms with the king and his fifth wife, Kathryn Howard.

▶ ② Hever Castle, given to Anne of Cleves after her marriage ended.

Anne's story

As a noblewoman, living in difficult times, I always knew that my parents would arrange a political match for me, but I was very surprised when I learned that someone as grand as the King of England wanted me to be his wife. Of course, I was honoured, although I was also worried. After all, everyone knew what had happened to his first two wives. So, before I left for England, I determined that I would always act as a good wife should. I would not get involved in politics and I would be honourable and good.

I was very excited to arrive in England, because I had not been away from my homeland before, but you can imagine my disappointment when Henry let everyone know how unhappy he was with me. I know I am not the prettiest of women, and in Cleve we do not use fancy perfumes to disguise our strong body odour, but I still thought that the king would be happy with me. I did not expect that Henry would try to break off our engagement and that after our marriage he would be unwilling to share our marriage bed, even for one night. I have to say that I did not find Henry attractive either, but all the same I was determined to be a faithful wife.

My life at court was very difficult. I had been raised to be a good wife and had not been taught music, singing or dancing, which many of the women at Henry's court knew well. I also did not speak any English, Latin or French, but I was famous for my skill at needlework, which made many people think highly of me, and I engaged a tutor to teach me English. I also made sure to never drink alcohol, or to give anyone a reason to tell tales about me.

continued...

Although the king did not want to be married to me, I played the good wife. I appeared at some public events, and spent my days playing cards with my ladies-in-waiting, learning English, and working on my needlework. I hoped that in time I could convince the king to have me crowned in a coronation and secure my place as queen.

Because I did not speak English well, I could not understand the gossip at court and it was several months before I heard the rumours of the king's interest in Kathryn Howard. I remembered what had happened to Catherine and Anne, and so when the king asked me to agree to an end to my marriage, I did it without hesitation. After all, it is better to be alive and not be queen, than to be dead.

But because I had never given the king any cause to dislike me, he rewarded my co-operation with a rank as the second lady in the kingdom after any future queen – even before the king's daughters. I was also given a rich collection of estates and manors that provided me with a handsome yearly income. I simply had to agree not to leave England. I was to bear the title of the 'King's Sister'. In this way the king kept the good connections of my family but was free to marry again. As for me, I was then 25, wealthy and free, something I soon learned to enjoy. You see, I had never been in love with the king, so I did not miss him.

I enjoyed a life of leisure and spent my time at cards, games and masques. I even learned to drink alcohol. I remained good friends with the king and his new wife, Kathryn Howard, and entertained them at dinner often. Of course, I never married again.

In her own words:

Letter from Anne of Cleves to Henry, 11 July, 1540.

This letter was written while the marriage was being set aside. It was intended to make Henry feel good and also get him on her side:

Pleaseth your most excellent majesty to understand that, whereas, at sundry times heretofore, I have been informed and perceived by certain lords and others your grace's council, of the doubts and questions which have been moved and found in our marriage; and how hath petition thereupon been made to your highness by your nobles and commons, that the same might be examined and determined by the holy clergy of this realm; to testify to your highness by my writing, that which I have before promised by my word and will, that is to say, that the matter should be examined and determined by the said clergy; it may please your majesty to know that, though this case must needs be most hard and sorrowful unto me, for the great love which I bear to your most noble person, yet, having more regard to God and his truth than to any worldly affection, as it beseemed me, at the beginning, to submit me to such examination and determination of the said clergy, whom I have and do accept for judges competent in that behalf. So now being ascertained how the same clergy hath therein given their judgment and sentence, I acknowledge myself hereby to accept and approve the same, wholly and entirely putting myself, for my state and condition, to your highness' goodness and pleasure; most humbly beseeching your majesty that, though it be determined that the pretended matrimony between us is void and of none effect, whereby I neither can nor will repute myself for your grace's wife, considering this sentence (whereunto I stand) and your majesty's clean and pure living with me, yet it will please you to take me for one of your humble servants, and so determine of me, as I may sometimes have the fruition of your most noble presence; which as I shall esteem for a great benefit, so, my lords and others of your majesty's council, now being with me, have put me in comfort thereof; and that your highness will take me for your sister; for the which I most humbly thank you accordingly.

Thus, most gracious prince, I beseech our Lord God to send your majesty long life and good health, to God's glory, your own honour, and the wealth of this noble realm.

From Richmond, the 11th day of July, the 32nd year of your majesty's most noble reign.

Your majesty's most humble sister and servant,

Anne the daughter of Cleves

Kathryn Howard

Young Kathryn could not keep her eyes off the young men. This was not a good idea when she was married to a jealous husband.

Kathryn Howard was the first cousin to Anne Boleyn, Henry's second queen. She was related to the Duke of Norfolk, but because her actual father was so poor, he asked Kathryn's step-grandmother to raise her. Unfortunately, no-one kept a close eye on Kathryn while she was growing up or explained to her that actions have consequences.

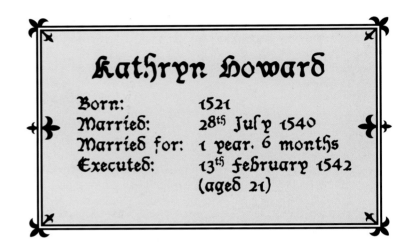

Kathryn Howard
Born: 1521
Married: 28ᵗʰ July 1540
Married for: 1 year, 6 months
Executed: 13ᵗʰ February 1542
             (aged 21)

When Kathryn (picture ①) arrived at court to be a maid-of-honour for Anne of Cleves, the king immediately fell wildly in love with her. She was not especially beautiful, but she was cheerful and made the now middle aged and ill king feel so much better. But she was not clever and was ignorant of the ways of the court. She continued to have love affairs that eventually broke Henry's heart which led to her downfall. People said that she was beautiful, kind-hearted and good-natured, but that all she cared about was dancing and merry-making.

Things were made worse by Kathryn's father, who was very keen on a marriage. He was a poor nobleman and he saw his daughter's wedding as a way of becoming more wealthy himself.

Soon, all of the court and London knew Henry's feelings, for the king was frequently seen being rowed in a small boat to Lambeth, where Kathryn lived at the home of her step-grandmother, the Dowager Duchess of Norfolk.

Henry gave Kathryn all the gifts he could – from diamonds and pearls to the estates once owned by Queen Jane. He also called her his "blushing rose without a thorn." But, of course, this was not what Kathryn really wanted. While courting the king, she actually wanted to fall in love with and marry a man of her own age (about 19).

Sixteen days after he was free of Anne, Henry, now fat, with a painful ulcerated leg and aged 49, married Kathryn Howard.

► ① Kathryn Howard had not learned how jealous her husband could be.

SVÆ ·21·

◀▲ ② The Tower of London and the executioner's block and axe.

Affairs

It took less than a year after the marriage for rumours to spread around the court that the new queen was having affairs with other men. This was extremely dangerous for any queen, but even more so for one who came from a powerful family because the Norfolks had many enemies.

Kathryn seems to have been unaware of all of this and she made one of her boyfriends her personal secretary.

Henry VIII, for once, did not suspect his wife of carrying on affairs behind his back. But it was in many people's interests to let the king know exactly what was going on. One of these was the Archbishop of Canterbury, Thomas Cranmer. He hated the Norfolks because they were Catholics. Cranmer had spies collect evidence against Kathryn and he then showed this to the king. Henry was stunned and had Kathryn confined to her apartments. Of course, after torture, plenty of evidence and confessions were to hand. When it was all shown to the king in November 1541 Henry broke down in tears and left Hampton Court Palace brokenhearted, never to see Queen Kathryn again.

Execution

The trial did not take long. Kathryn was beheaded outside the Tower of London on 13 February, 1542 and buried near the body of her cousin Anne Boleyn who had been executed for the same reasons just a few years before (picture ②).

Kathryn's story

My parents came from a noble and powerful family. But not all of my family were rich. In fact my father was poor because he was a younger son of the Duke of Norfolk, not the heir to the family fortune. This is why, at an early age, I was sent to live with my step-grandmother, Agnes, Dowager Duchess of Norfolk. The Duchess of Norfolk had been a very important woman at court when she was younger and my parents hoped that she would help me to win the heart of a wealthy young nobleman with good connections.

The Duchess had a lovely and comfortable house at Lambeth near London and she arranged for me to learn to read, write and to play music – important skills at Henry's court. She was not very strict, so I was able to do the things I loved best – flirt with boys and make merry. In fact, I made merry with two much older men while I lived with the Duchess and she never knew.

When I was 15, the Duchess arranged for me to start my life at court as maid-of-honour to Anne of Cleves. I loved life at court. It was so glamorous and luxurious and there were so many handsome men! But the court was home to the king. It was not long before he caught my eye, or was it the other way around? I don't remember. He was certainly not young or handsome, but fat and with an ulcerated leg. I did not mind, because he was king and he gave me all sorts of wonderful and beautiful gifts. All I had to do was laugh and flirt and I knew that I could be queen.

But being queen was not as much fun as I thought it would be. I cared for Henry and we had fun together, even though he was old and the ulcer on his leg was a bit disgusting and smelly.

continued...

When Henry was sad and cross, I dutifully attended him. I ignored the pus-oozing ulcers on his leg and he rewarded me with his love and with many gifts.

I did not meddle in Henry's political affairs and had no interest in religious issues. I was really only interested in having fun, and with so many young men around, there were so many opportunities.

Eventually, I was found out. It was one of my family's enemies, Archbishop Cranmer, who told the king about my affairs. He hated my family because we are Catholics and he is a Reformer and he was always looking for evidence against me. I suppose it wasn't too hard to find (see my letter below). At first, I hoped the king would forgive me, but there was too much evidence. At first, I panicked, but then decided that I would at least die with dignity.

The night before my execution I had the executioner's block brought to me so that I could rehearse for my final appearance as queen. Throughout the night, I practised placing my head on the block, for I was determined to die with dignity and composure. Although so weak I could barely stand, I managed to make a short speech in which I admitted I was justly condemned, prayed for the king and asked for God's mercy.

In her own words:

Letter from Queen Kathryn Howard to Thomas Culpepper Spring 1541.

Only eight months after being married to Henry, Kathryn was making love to Thomas Culpepper. Legend has it that Kathryn's last words were:

"I die a queen, but would rather die the wife of Culpepper."

Master Culpepper,

I heartily recommend me unto you, praying you to send me word how that you do. It was showed me that you was sick, the which thing troubled me very much till such time that I hear from you praying you to send me word how that you do, for I never longed so much for a thing as I do to see you and to speak with you, the which I trust shall be shortly now. That which doth comfort me very much when I think of it, and when I think again that you shall depart from me again it makes my heart die to think what fortune I have that I cannot be always in your company. It my trust is always in you that you will be as you have promised me, and in that hope I trust upon still, praying you that you will come when my Lady Rochford is here for then I shall be best at leisure to be at your commandment, thanking you for that you have promised me to be so good unto that poor fellow my man which is one of the griefs that I do feel to depart from him for then I do know no one that I dare trust to send to you, and therefore I pray you take him to be with you that I may sometime hear from you one thing. I pray you to give me a horse for my man for I had much ado to get one and therefore I pray send me one by him and in so doing I am as I said afore, and thus I take my leave of you, trusting to see you shortly again and I would you was with me now that you might see what pain I take in writing to you.

Yours as long as life endures,

Kathryn

One thing I had forgotten and that is to instruct my man to tarry here with me still for he says whatsomever you bid him he will do it.

Katherine Parr (Katharine Parre)

Katherine Parr was of a similar age to Henry's older daughter and she was almost like a niece to him – until he fell in love.

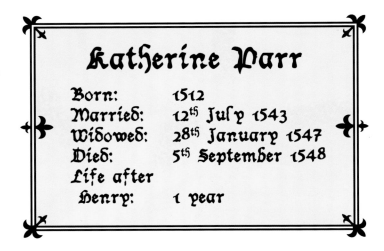

Katherine Parr

Born:	1512
Married:	12th July 1543
Widowed:	28th January 1547
Died:	5th September 1548
Life after Henry:	1 year

Katherine Parr was the sixth and the last of Henry's wives (picture ①). Katherine was not the daughter of a king or powerful noble. Instead, she was the daughter of a modest country squire who had served Henry VIII when he was young.

Katherine's mother was a lady-in-waiting to Catherine of Aragon and it may have been that Katherine grew up and was taught with Princess Mary, the king's eldest daughter. Mary was just four years younger than Katherine.

Katherine at court

Katherine was used to court circles and she learned French and Italian, could read and write in Latin and Greek. She was naturally very bright. Because it was quite unusual for women to be highly educated in Tudor times, this set Katherine apart from others at court. Katherine was a Reformer (Protestant) and one of her favourite pastimes was to debate religious issues.

Henry was actually Katherine's third husband, the first two having died. How the king hit on the idea of marrying Katherine Parr is not recorded, but, of course, he had known her since she was a child playing with his own children.

Queen and nurse

As the king was in the last stages of life, it was not an attractive proposition marrying him. In any case, most of those at court with eligible daughters were not keen on putting them forward because of what had happened to Henry's previous wives. Besides, there were few women of marriageable age without faults that could be brought to the king's notice by their enemies.

So, a sensible widow was just the thing for Henry. She was religious, she was dependable, she could hold a good conversation with Henry (remember that Henry was, himself, a very intelligent man).

THARINE PARRE

▶ ① Katherine Parr was Henry's last wife.

Henry and Katherine Parr were married at Hampton Court Palace on 12 July, 1543, about 18 months after Kathryn Howard's execution.

Henry's eldest daughter Mary was still a Catholic and she had not been on speaking terms with Henry, his son and other daughter Elizabeth (who were all Reformers). Katherine spent time and effort bringing the family back together.

Katherine was not involved with power struggles or lovers and so royal family life became more settled than it had ever been. In fact, she knew exactly how to be a traditional queen.

Katherine also used her position and cleverness to make it more acceptable for women to be educated. She even wrote books including *Prayers and Meditations.*

Dependable Katherine

Henry was not quite finished yet. He embarked on an invasion of France in 1544. He thought so much of Katherine's ability that he made her regent (the person who takes on the powers of the king) while he was away.

Trouble afoot

But even for a smart, loyal queen, it was not all plain sailing. There were other religious leaders who saw Katherine as an obstacle in their way to power. One of the bishops, Stephen Gardiner, warned Henry against harbouring "a serpent within his own bosom." His suspicions aroused, Henry listened, then signed a warrant for Katherine's arrest on grounds of **HERESY**. The queen's ladies immediately threw away banned books on religion, while Katherine hastened to the king.

Henry said to Katherine, "ye are become a doctor, Kate, to instruct us . . ." But this time Katherine had the perfect response: "I am but a woman, with all the imperfections natural to the weakness of my sex; therefore in all matters of doubt and difficulty I must refer myself to your Majesty's better judgement, as to my lord and head." The plan worked. Queen Katherine was given a set of new jewels. Her approach had saved her life.

After Henry

Katherine outlived Henry, who died on 28 January, 1547. On his deathbed, Henry instructed that Katherine should be given £7,000 each year (a vast sum at the time) and be allowed to keep all her jewels.

Prince Edward succeeded Henry VIII as Edward VI. His older uncle, Edward Seymour, Lord Somerset, became Protector since the young king was not yet 10 years old.

The other Seymour brother, Thomas, wanted to marry Katherine Parr, and this time she was free to accept (picture ②).

Katherine was soon pregnant with Seymour's child, and gave birth to a daughter named Mary on 30 August, 1548. Unfortunately, Katherine did not recover from the childbirth and died on 5 September.

◀ ② **Sir Thomas Seymour.**

Katherine's story

I had never expected to be queen, especially at the late age of 31, and already twice married and widowed. But Henry and I had known each other since I was a child. My father and Henry were old friends and I think he turned to me as a trusted and true nursemaid. When Henry asked me to marry him, I already had a marriage understanding with Sir Thomas Seymour, younger brother of the late Queen Jane. But I put aside love for duty, for when the king asks for your hand in marriage, it does not do to say no.

My duty as queen was clear, to play nurse to the king and to act as a traditional queen – speaking with ambassadors, entertaining at court, and setting an example for the people by being trustworthy and true. In truth, the king was not demanding of me, I was not expected to have any children, but to be a companion to the king. I also took Henry's children under my care. They had too long been denied a mother's love and care, and I was anxious that they did not grow up wild because of this.

I had been brought up as a Protestant and I hoped that my time at court would influence the king and country more in that direction. I had been given a great deal of education by my mother, more than most women receive, and I was used to leading scholarly debates.

continued...

Unfortunately, the king was tired and had lost interest in church reform and I fell foul of Lord Chancellor Thomas Wriothesley, and his campaign to wipe out so-called "heretics". Wriothesley led a conservative group who wished to turn the country back towards Catholicism and they saw me as an obstacle to this.

The king and I often passed the time in religious discussion and one day the anti-reform Bishop Stephen Gardiner, a firm friend of Wriothesley, overheard a most vigorous religious argument between us. Gardiner warned Henry against harbouring "a serpent within his own bosom," and convinced Henry to sign a warrant for my arrest on grounds of heresy.

A servant loyal to me gave me a copy of the warrant. At first I panicked, and then I realised what I had to do to survive. While my ladies-in-waiting burned all the banned books on religion I had collected in my room, I hurried to the king.

Henry steered the conversation to religion, commenting that "ye are become a doctor, Kate, to instruct us . . .," but I had the perfect response. I replied, "I am but a woman, with all the imperfections natural to the weakness of my sex; therefore in all matters of doubt and difficulty I must refer myself to your Majesty's better judgement, as to my lord and head".

My submissiveness worked. When that fool Wriothesley next came to see the king, he was greeted with cries from the king of "Knave!," "Fool!" and "Beast!" The warrant was dropped and I was given a set of gorgeous new jewels for my loyalty.

When the king died, I was sad, for he had been a good husband to me, but I had done my duty and my life at court was over. Once my period of mourning was over, I was free to marry Seymour and once again live my own life.

KATHERINE PARR

In her own words:

Letter from Katherine Parr to Henry VIII, July 1544.

While Henry VIII invaded France in 1544, Katherine Parr acted as regent. Katherine knew how suspicious the old king could be, and so she made sure she included lots of humble and loyal words.

Although the distance of time and account of days neither is long nor many of your majesty's absence, yet the want of your presence, so much desired and beloved by me, maketh me that I cannot quietly pleasure in anything until I hear from your majesty. The time, therefore, seemeth to me very long, with a great desire to know how your highness hath done since your departing hence, whose prosperity and health I prefer and desire more than mine own. And whereas I know your majesty's absence is never without great need, yet love and affection compel me to desire your presence.

Again, the same zeal and affection force me to be best content with that which is your will and pleasure. Thus love maketh me in all things to set apart mine own convenience and pleasure, and to embrace most joyfully his will and pleasure whom I love. God, the knower of secrets, can judge these words not to be written only with ink, but most truly impressed on the heart. Much more I omit, lest it be thought I go about to praise myself, or crave a thank; which thing to do I mind nothing less, but a plain, simple relation of the love and zeal I bear your majesty, proceeding from the abundance of the heart. Wherein I must confess I desire no commendation, having such just occasion to do the same. I make like account with your majesty as I do with God for his benefits and gifts heaped upon me daily, acknowledging myself a great debtor to him, not being able to recompense the least of his benefits; in which state I am certain and sure to die, yet I hope in His gracious acceptation of my goodwill. Even such confidence have I in your majesty's gentleness, knowing myself never to have done my duty as were requisite and meet for such a noble prince, at whose hands I have found and received so much love and goodness, that with words I cannot express it. Lest I should be too tedious to your majesty, I finish this my scribbled letter, committing you to the governance of the Lord with long and prosperous life here, and after this life to enjoy the kingdom of his elect.

From Greenwich, by your majesty's humble and obedient servant,

Katherine the Queen.

Tudor wives' timeline

1529 Henry VIII dismisses Lord Chancellor Thomas Wolsey for failing to obtain the Pope's consent to his divorce from **Catherine of Aragon**.

1533 Henry VIII marries **Anne Boleyn** and is excommunicated by Pope Clement VII.

Sir Thomas More appointed Lord Chancellor.

Henry VIII summons the "Reformation Parliament" and begins to cut the ties with the Church of Rome.

Thomas Cranmer appointed Archbishop of Canterbury.

11 June 1509 Henry VIII marries Catherine of Aragon.

1510   1520   1530

1509 Henry VIII, becomes king.

1532 Sir Thomas More resigns over the question of Henry VIII's divorce.

1534 Act of Supremacy: Henry VIII declared supreme head of the Church of England.

1536 Anne Boleyn is beheaded.

Henry VIII marries **Jane Seymour**.

Dissolution of monasteries in England begins under the direction of Thomas Cromwell, completed in 1539.

1540 Henry VIII marries **Anne of Cleves** following negotiations by Thomas Cromwell.

Henry divorces **Anne of Cleves** and marries **Kathryn Howard**.

Thomas Cromwell executed on charge of treason.

1542 Kathryn Howard is executed.

1543 Henry VIII marries **Katherine Parr**.

Alliance between Henry and Charles V (Holy Roman Emperor) against Scotland and France.

1540

1550

1547 Henry VIII dies, Edward VI becomes king.

1535 Sir Thomas More is beheaded in Tower of London for failing to take the Oath of Supremacy.

1537 Jane Seymour dies after the birth of a son, the future Edward VI.

1539 Dissolution of Glastonbury Abbey; buildings torched and looted by the king's men.

Abbot Richard Whiting is executed by hanging atop Glastonbury Tor.

Glossary

ADULTERY Making love to a husband or wife to whom you are not married.

CATHOLIC, ROMAN CATHOLIC Part of the Christian Church whose head is the Pope in Rome.

CIVIL WAR A war between two groups of people who belong to the same country. Usually a civil war is a fight over who should succeed to the throne.

CONVENT A religious house for nuns. Nuns are said to be married to Christ and so cannot also be married to a man.

DOWRY The money paid to the husband's family by the wife's father.

HERESY Something said or written against the teachings of the church.

MISCARRIAGE When a mother has a baby that is born dead. This usually happens when the baby is very small and long before it would normally have been born.

MISTRESS A women who is not married to a man, but who is almost like a second wife. However, a mistress is never openly acknowledged.

NOBLE People who belonged to rich and powerful families and who had titles given by the king.

PREGNANT To carry a child.

PRIVY COUNCIL The group of most senior government ministers.

REFORMERS People who thought that the Catholic Church had lost its way and become too much to do with ritual. They were also called Protestants because they protested against the way the Catholic Church behaved.

TREASON Doing something which will threaten the country's welfare. In Tudor times the country was the king.

TUDOR The kings and queens who made up the royal line starting with Henry VII and ending with Elizabeth I (because she was childless).

Index

Introduction

This revision guide is matched to the new single award **OCR GCSE Science A specification (J630)**, from the **Twenty First Century Science Suite**. As such, it provides

Stage 4 Program

The guide is des
language of the
framework of **Sc**
biology, chemistr
concepts, called
concerned with t
to develop scient
that arise when s
practical use.

As a revision guic
and material on v
covers the **nine n**
Context; it does
analysis and case
your science teach

You will have to s
overview of these
details of where th
in this guide:

• The **contents l**
  guide clearly ide
  help you revise
  the pages are **colour coded** so that you can
  easily distinguish between biology, chemistry and
  physics content.

• The **Ideas in Context** paper will focus on three of the modules you have already studied (one each from biology, chemistry and physics). It will ...anding of the content and your ...at knowledge, for example, to ...ion about a current social- ...paper is looked at in more ...7–92.

...be used to revise for both the ...Higher Tier exam papers. ...ll only be tested on the ...pers appears in a coloured box, ...y identified by the symbol **HT**.

...module there is a **summary** ...s all the key Scientific ...Ideas About Science. These ...as checklists to help you with ...e sure you are familiar with all ...d ideas listed – they are ...erstanding of the material in

...**sary** at the back, providing ...essential words and phrases, ...**eriodic table** for reference.

...ormation in this guide – ...wn anything you think will ...help you to remember and constantly test yourself without looking at the text.

Good luck with your exams!

Title	What is Being Assessed?	Duration	Weighting	Total Mark	Page Numbers
Unit 1	Modules B1, C1 and P1	40 minutes	16.7%	42	Pages 6–32
Unit 2	Modules B2, C2 and P2	40 minutes	16.7%	42	Pages 33–57
Unit 3	Modules B3, C3 and P3	40 minutes	16.7%	42	Pages 58–86
Unit 4	Ideas in Context	45 minutes	16.7%	40	Pages 87–92

Acknowledgements

Acknowledgements

Author Information

Dr Dorothy Warren is a member of the Royal Society of Chemistry, a former science teacher, and a Secondary Science Consultant with the Curriculum & Management Advisory Service for North Yorkshire County Council. Having been involved in the pilot scheme for Twenty First Century Science, she has an excellent understanding of the new specifications, which she is helping to implement in local schools.

Dr Eliot Attridge is a full member of the Institute of Biology, a chartered biologist CBiol, and an experienced Head of Science. He works closely with the exam board as an Assistant Examiner for Twenty First Century Science and was involved in writing the scheme of work for the new GCSE. His school, having been involved in the pilot, is now implementing the new GCSE.

Nathan Goodman has an in-depth understanding of the new science specifications, thanks to his roles as Secondary Science Strategy Consultant for North East Lincolnshire LEA and Regional Coordinator at the Institute of Physics for the physics teacher network. A former teacher himself, he is involved in designing and delivering INSET to teachers and supporting them in their own schools.

Project Editor: Charlotte Christensen
Editor: Rebecca Skinner
Cover and concept design: Sarah Duxbury
Designer: Ian Wrigley

ISBN 978-1-905129-59-1

Published by Lonsdale, a division of Huveaux Plc.

The authors and publisher would like to thank everyone who contributed images to this book:

IFC	©iStockphoto.com / Andrei Tchernov
p.8	©iStockphoto.com / Linda Bucklin
p.12	©iStockphoto.com / Patrick Hermans
p.19	©iStockphoto.com / Mohamad Saipul Nang
p.19	©iStockphoto.com / Helle Bro Clemmensen
p.21	©iStockphoto.com / Luis Carlos Torres
p.29	NASA
p.31	©iStockphoto.com / Steve O'connor
p.33	©iStockphoto.com
p.33	©iStockphoto.com / Konstantinos Kokkinis
p.33	©iStockphoto.com / Linda Bucklin
p.35	©iStockphoto.com
p.38	©iStockphoto.com / Peter Galbraith
p.48	©iStockphoto.com / Tim Dalek
p.55	©iStockphoto.com / Brandon Laufenberg
p.56	©iStockphoto.com / Marc Dietrich
p.58	©iStockphoto.com / Christian Darkin
p.59	©iStockphoto.com / Linda Bucklin
p.71	©iStockphoto.com / Paul IJsendoorn
p.72	©iStockphoto.com / Jolande Gerritsen
p.75	©iStockphoto.com / Yale Bernstein
p.76	©iStockphoto.com
p.87	©iStockphoto.com / Stefan Klein
p.92	©iStockphoto.com / Frank Tschakert

Artwork supplied by HL Studios

Data on p.20 provided by Pfizer

Data on p.46 provided by *Disposable Nappies: a case study in waste prevention*, © Women's Environmental Network, April 2003; www.wen.org.uk

Contents

Contents

You and Your Genes

Many of an individual's characteristics are inherited from their two biological parents. This module looks at…

- genes, and their effect on development
- why family members can resemble each other but are not identical
- how genetic information can, and should, be used
- how an understanding of genetics can prevent disease
- stem cells, and their role in treating disease.

Variation

Differences between individuals of the same species are described as **variations**.

Variation may be due to...

- **genes** – the different characteristics an individual inherits, e.g. the colour of dogs' coats
- **environment** – the conditions in which an individual develops, e.g. how much someone weighs.

Genetic causes

Environmental causes

Usually variation is due to a **combination** of genetic and environmental causes.

Genetic Information

Genes carry the information needed for an individual organism to develop. Different genes control the development of different characteristics, e.g. eye colour. Genes occur in long strings called **chromosomes**. These are located inside the **nucleus** of every cell in the organism.

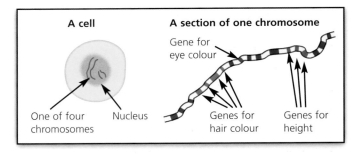

Chromosomes are made of **DNA** (deoxyribonucleic acid) molecules. Each DNA molecule consists of two strands, which are coiled to form a **double helix**. The DNA molecules form a complete set of instructions for how the organism should be constructed and how its individual cells should function.

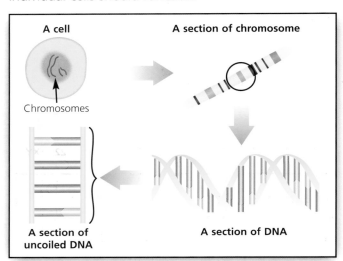

Genes are sections of DNA. They control the development of different characteristics by issuing instructions to the cell. The cell carries out these instructions by producing **proteins**.

HT The proteins formed inside a cell are either **structural proteins** (used for cell growth or repair) or **enzymes**. Enzymes speed up chemical reactions in cells but are not used up in the process.

Genetic Modification

All organisms have DNA. This means it is possible to introduce genetic information from one organism into another organism to produce a new combination of genes and characteristics. This process is called **genetic modification**.

You and Your Genes

Chromosomes

Chromosomes normally come in **pairs**. Both chromosomes in a pair have the same sequence of genes, i.e. the same genes in the same place. Different species have different numbers of pairs. **Human cells** contain **23 pairs** of chromosomes (46 in total).

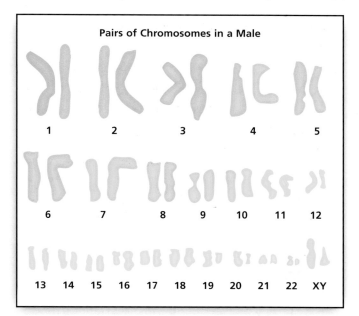

Pairs of Chromosomes in a Male

1   2   3   4   5

6   7   8   9   10   11   12

13   14   15   16   17   18   19   20   21   22   XY

The **sex cells,** eggs produced by the **ovaries** in females and sperm produced by the **testes** in males, contain single chromosomes. They have a total of 23 chromosomes; half the number of a normal body cell.

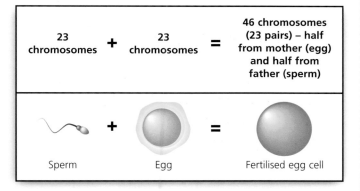

| 23 chromosomes + 23 chromosomes = | 46 chromosomes (23 pairs) – half from mother (egg) and half from father (sperm) |

Sperm + Egg = Fertilised egg cell

Alleles

A gene can have different versions, called **alleles**. For example, the gene for eye colour has two alleles: brown and blue. Similarly, the gene for tongue rolling has two alleles: being able to roll your tongue and not being able to roll your tongue.

For each gene, an individual inherits one allele from their father and one allele from their mother. (This is why individuals can have similarities to both of their parents.) An individual can inherit two alleles that are the same or two alleles that are different. The process is completely **random**. Siblings (brothers and sisters) can inherit different combinations of alleles for all the different genes, which is why they can be very different.

Alleles are described as being either **dominant** or **recessive**. A dominant allele is one which controls the development of a characteristic even if it is present on only one chromosome in a pair. A recessive allele is one which controls the development of a characteristic only if a dominant allele is not present, i.e. if the recessive allele is present on both chromosomes in a pair.

Genetic Diagrams

Genetic diagrams are used to show all the possible combinations of alleles and outcomes for a particular gene. They use **capital letters for dominant alleles** and **lower case letters for recessive alleles**.

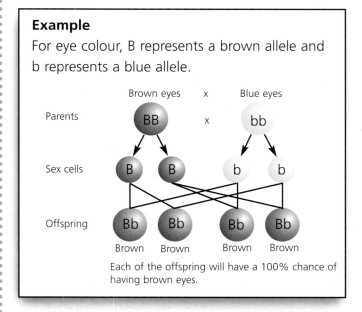

Example
For eye colour, B represents a brown allele and b represents a blue allele.

Brown eyes   x   Blue eyes

Parents   BB   x   bb

Sex cells   B   B   b   b

Offspring   Bb   Bb   Bb   Bb
Brown   Brown   Brown   Brown

Each of the offspring will have a 100% chance of having brown eyes.

Family trees can also be used to identify how an individual has inherited a characteristic, like blue eye colour or not being able to roll their tongue.

You and Your Genes

Genetics and Lifestyle

Most characteristics are determined by several genes working together, however, they can also be influenced by environmental factors.

For example, height is determined by a variety of genes, but factors like diet can also affect how tall an individual grows.

Factors like poor diet can also lead to disease, e.g. a fatty diet can increase the risk of heart disease.

So, it is possible to limit the chances of getting certain diseases and disorders by making lifestyle changes.

Sex Chromosomes

One of the 23 pairs of chromosomes in a human cell is the sex chromosomes. In females the **sex chromosomes** are identical; they are both **X chromosomes**. In males they are different; there is an **X** and a **Y chromosome**. The Y chromosome is much shorter than the X chromosome.

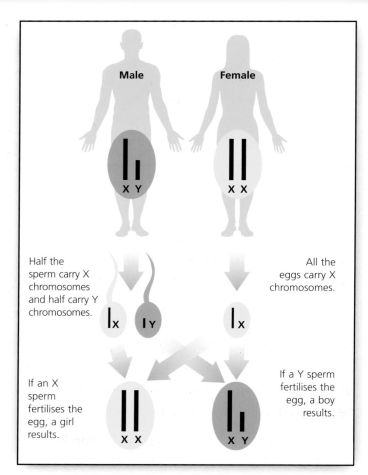

Male   Female

X Y   X X

Half the sperm carry X chromosomes and half carry Y chromosomes.

All the eggs carry X chromosomes.

X   Y   X

If an X sperm fertilises the egg, a girl results.

If a Y sperm fertilises the egg, a boy results.

X X   X Y

Sex Determination

The sex of an individual is determined by a gene on the Y chromosome called the SRY (sex-determining region Y) gene.

If the gene is not present, i.e. if there are two X chromosomes present, the embryo will develop into a female. If the gene is present, i.e. if there are an X and a Y chromosome, testes begin to develop.

After six weeks the testes start producing a hormone called **androgen**. Specialised receptors in the developing embryo detect the androgen and male reproductive organs begin to grow.

Sometimes the Y chromosome is present but androgen is *not* detected. When this happens, the embryo develops female sex organs apart from the uterus. The baby is born with a female body but is infertile.

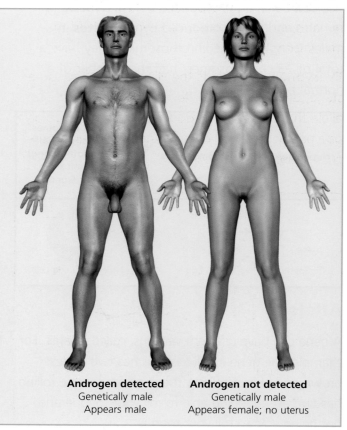

Androgen detected
Genetically male
Appears male

Androgen not detected
Genetically male
Appears female; no uterus

You and Your Genes

Rare Disorders

Most characteristics are governed by a range of genes, so the presence of one 'faulty' allele may not affect the overall outcome.

However, although rare, there are some disorders which are caused by a single allele, e.g. **Huntington's disorder**.

Huntington's Disorder

Huntington's disorder (HD), is a genetic disorder that affects the **central nervous system**. It is caused by a 'faulty' gene on the fourth pair of chromosomes.

The HD gene results in damage to the nerve cells in certain areas of the brain. This causes gradual physical, mental and emotional changes, which develop into continuous, involuntary movement and dementia. The **symptoms** can differ from person to person, even within the same family.

The initial symptoms of HD normally develop in adulthood, which means sufferers may already have had children and passed on the gene. There is no cure, so the disorder will eventually lead to premature death.

Everyone who inherits the HD gene will, at some stage, develop the disorder. This is because the allele that causes HD is **dominant**. Therefore, only *one* parent needs to pass on the faulty gene for a child to inherit the disorder.

Cystic Fibrosis

Cystic fibrosis is the UK's most common life-threatening **genetic disorder**. It affects the cell membranes, causing a **thick**, **sticky** mucus, especially in the **lungs**, **gut** and **pancreas**.

Symptoms of cystic fibrosis can include weight loss, troublesome coughs, repeated chest infections, salty sweat and abnormal faeces.

Although there is no cure at present, scientists have identified the allele that causes it and are looking for ways to repair or replace it.

Unlike Huntington's disorder, the cystic fibrosis allele is **recessive**. Therefore, if an individual has *one* recessive allele, they *will not* have the characteristics associated with the disorder. However, they are called **carriers** because they can pass the allele on to their children.

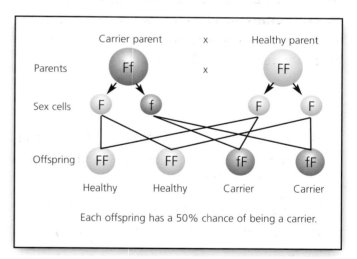

Each offspring has a 50% chance of being a carrier.

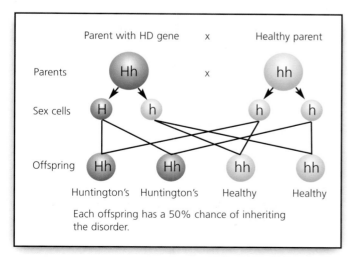

Each offspring has a 50% chance of inheriting the disorder.

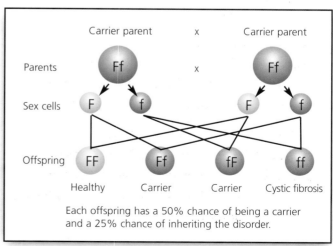

Each offspring has a 50% chance of being a carrier and a 25% chance of inheriting the disorder.

You and Your Genes

Genetic Testing

It is now possible to test individuals for a 'faulty' allele if there is a family history of a genetic disorder. If the tests turn out to be positive, the individual will have to decide whether or not to have children and risk passing on the disorder. Possible alternatives include adoption or embryo selection (see p.11).

Fetuses can also be tested. However, if a developing baby is found to have the faulty allele, the parents then have to decide whether or not to terminate the pregnancy (have an abortion). These decisions can be very difficult and traumatic.

Testing the Fetus

There are two types of genetic test that can be carried out on a fetus.

1 Amniocentesis Testing

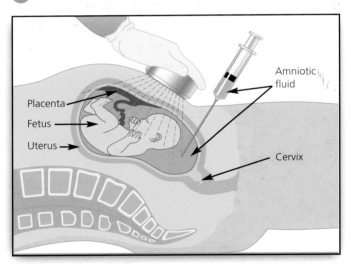

This test can be carried out at 14–16 weeks of pregnancy. A needle is inserted into the uterus, taking care to avoid the fetus and a small sample of amniotic fluid, which carries cells from the fetus, is extracted.

Results take up to two weeks to return. If the test is positive for a given disorder the pregnancy (now at 16–18 weeks) could be terminated. There is a 0.5% chance of the test causing a miscarriage, i.e. 1 in every 200 tests. There is also a very small chance of infection.

2 Chorionic Villus Testing

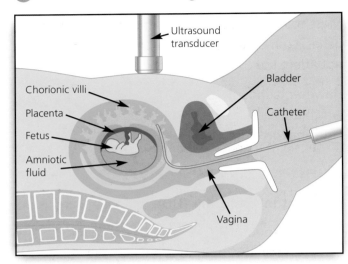

This test is carried out earlier, at 8–10 weeks of pregnancy. A special catheter is inserted through the vagina and cervix until it reaches the placenta. Part of the placenta has chorionic villi (finger-like protrusions), which are made from fetal cells. Samples are removed for testing.

Results take up to two weeks to return. If the test is positive for a given disorder the pregnancy can be terminated much earlier (10–12 weeks) than with amniocentesis testing. However, the chance of a miscarriage is much higher at 2%, i.e. 1 in every 50 tests. There is virtually no risk of infection.

Reliability

Because no test is 100% reliable, genetic testing on a fetus can have a number of possible outcomes:

Outcome	Test result	Reality
True Positive	Fetus Has the disorder	Fetus has the disorder
True Negative	Fetus does not have the disorder	Fetus does not have the disorder
False Positive	Fetus has the disorder	Fetus **does not** have the disorder
False Negative	Fetus does not have the disorder	Fetus **has** the disorder

False negatives are rare and false positives are even rarer. However, the consequence of a false positive is that the parents may choose to terminate the pregnancy when the embryo is in fact healthy.

The Implications of Genetic Testing

There are lots of questions that need to be addressed before genetic testing can become common practice. For example:

- How can we prevent mistakes from being made?
- Is it right to interfere with nature in this way?
- How can we decide, and who has the right to decide, if a genetic disorder is worth living with?

There is always a difference between what **can** be done (i.e. what is technically possible) and what **should** be done (i.e. what is morally acceptable). For example, governments may have the ability to genetically test individuals, but should they be allowed to do so?

Potentially, genetic testing could be used to produce detailed genetic profiles. These could contain information on everything from an individual's ethnicity to whether they are susceptible to certain conditions (e.g. obesity) or diseases (e.g. cancer).

It has been suggested that all babies could be screened at birth, allowing doctors to tailor healthcare for the individual and take action to prevent problems before they occur. The information could also help to stop genetic disorders from being passed on, eventually eliminating them from the population completely.

One view is that this would be a good thing; there would be less suffering and money currently spent on treating the disorders could be used elsewhere. Another view is that these disorders are natural and that it would be wrong to eliminate them.

The storage of genetic information also raises questions about confidentiality. There are concerns that without tight laws and regulations in place, companies could use the information to discriminate against individuals,

e.g. an individual might be turned down for a job or refused insurance because they have a high risk of getting cancer or heart disease.

Different cultures and societies will have different needs and views on the subject. Because the availability of resources (e.g. money and trained personnel) affects what can be done, different countries also need to develop different policies towards genetic testing depending on their economy.

Embryo Selection

Embryo selection is another way of preventing babies from being born with genetic disorders.

Embryos can be produced by *in vitro* **fertilisation** (IVF). This is when ova (egg cells) are **harvested** from the mother, and fertilised in a laboratory using the father's sperm. The embryos are tested to see if they have a 'faulty' allele. Only the healthy ones are implanted into the mother's uterus, and the pregnancy then proceeds as normal.

The procedure for embryo selection is called **Pre-implantation Genetic Diagnosis (PGD)**.

After fertilisation, the embryos are allowed to divide into 8 cells before a single cell is removed from each one for another testing. The cells are tested to see if they carry the alleles for a specific genetic disorder, i.e. the disorder that one of the parents carries or has.

Embryo selection is controversial. Some people disagree with it because they believe it is unnatural. There are also concerns that people could start using this method to select the characteristics (such as eye colour, sex and IQ) of their baby in advance.

If this is allowed to happen it could reduce variation in humans. For example, if most people selected blue eyes, the brown eye allele could eventually disappear from the population.

You and Your Genes

Gene Therapy

Gene therapy is a potential new treatment for certain genetic disorders. It involves inserting 'healthy' genes into an individual's cells to treat a disease.

The most common method uses genes from healthy individuals. They are inserted into a modified virus, which infects the patient. The genes become incorporated into the patient's cells, correcting the faulty allele.

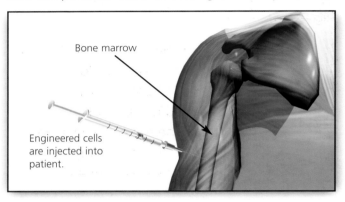

Bone marrow

Engineered cells are injected into patient.

New scientific procedures, like gene therapy, always raise lots of questions:

- Does it work and is it safe?
- What are the potential risks and side effects?
- How do you target the cells that need gene therapy?
- Can gene therapy cause cancer?

These questions can be answered by conducting further scientific research, however, there are some questions that cannot be answered by science:

- Is it right to manipulate genes in this way?
- Where do we draw the line between repairing damage and making improvements?
- Do we have the right to decide for future generations?

These examples are all asking the same basic question: **is gene therapy acceptable**? This is an **ethical** question. To answer it we need to make a value judgement, i.e. decide what is right and wrong.

Society is underpinned by a common belief system. For this reason, there are certain actions that can never be justified. For example, most people agree that theft and murder is wrong.

However, science can be a grey area. Individuals are influenced by different beliefs and experiences, so there are always lots of different views about what is acceptable, and what should be done.

An important question that is in dispute and needs to be settled is called an **issue**. There are lots of different views on most issues. Here are just a few for **gene therapy**:

For
<ul><li>It is an acceptable medical procedure, comparable to giving a vaccination, and is less invasive than surgery.</li><li>People with genetic conditions often require a lifetime of care and treatment. Gene therapy will improve their lives and will free up resources so they can be used elsewhere.</li><li>Some genetic conditions reduce life expectancy. Gene therapy will allow sufferers to enjoy a full and normal life.</li></ul>
Against
<ul><li>It is unnatural, and therefore morally wrong, to change people's genes and DNA.</li><li>It is an experimental treatment and we do not know what the long-term effects might be.</li><li>It will need to be tested on humans, which is not safe because we do not know what the side effects are.</li></ul>

An individual cannot decide whether gene therapy is right or wrong by simply counting up the arguments for and against. Each argument will have a different weighting depending on how important it is to them. For example, they might believe that it is far more important to save lives than to worry about the procedure being unnatural.

Because of all the different views, any decisions made by authorities (e.g. governments) over ethical issues are normally based on what will benefit the majority of people involved. Of course, this means there will always be some people who object.

Asexual Reproduction

Bacteria and other single-cell organisms can reproduce by dividing to form two 'new' individuals. The new individuals are **clones** (they are genetically **identical** to the parent).

This method of reproduction is called **asexual reproduction**. Most plants and some animals can also reproduce in this way.

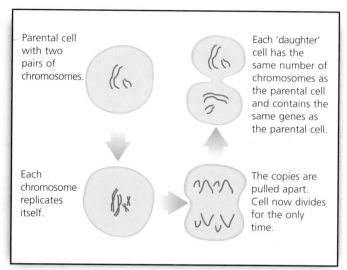

Parental cell with two pairs of chromosomes.

Each 'daughter' cell has the same number of chromosomes as the parental cell and contains the same genes as the parental cell.

Each chromosome replicates itself.

The copies are pulled apart. Cell now divides for the only time.

Variation in organisms that reproduce asexually is normally caused by **environmental factors**.

Clones

Clones of animals and humans can occur **naturally**. The cells of an embryo sometimes separate and the two new embryos develop into **identical twins**.

> **HT** Animal clones can also be produced **artificially**. The nucleus from an adult body cell is transferred into an empty (nucleus removed) unfertilised egg cell. The new individual will therefore have exactly the same genetic information as the donor.

Stem Cells

Most organisms are made up of lots of different **specialised** cells, which have different structures to help them perform their particular jobs.

In the initial stages of development, the cells in an embryo are not yet specialised; they are all the same. These are called **stem cells** and they have the potential to develop into virtually any type of body cell.

Stem cells can potentially be used to replace tissues that are damaged, e.g. they can be inserted into the brain of a patient with Parkinson's disease to replace the cells affected by the disease and alleviate the symptoms.

To produce the large number of stem cells needed for such treatments, it is necessary to clone embryos. The stem cells are collected when the embryo is five days old and made up of approximately 150 cells. The rest of the embryo is destroyed. At the moment, unused embryos from IVF treatments are used for stem cell research.

The Ethical Issue

There is an **issue** as to whether it is right to clone embryos and extract stem cells in this way. The debate revolves around whether or not these embryos should be treated as people. If they should, then using embryos in this way is obviously wrong. If they should not, then the procedure is acceptable.

One view is that if an embryo is produced for IVF treatment but is not used for implantation, it no longer has a future. Therefore, it is acceptable to use it for stem cell research as long as the mother and father have given consent.

However, if these embryos were not available, it has been suggested that embryos could be cloned from the patient's own cells. This is the first stage in **reproductive cloning** (the production of a new individual who is genetically identical to the donor), which is currently illegal in the UK.

The Government makes laws on issues like this with the guidance of special advisory committees, who are responsible for exploring the ethics of such procedures.

You and Your Genes – Summary

Science Explanations

Cells

- Most organisms are made up of specialised cells, which have different structures to help them perform a specific function.

Gene Theory

- Most animals and plants reproduce by sexual reproduction.
- During sexual reproduction a male sex cell joins with a female sex cell to form a fertilised egg.
- Variation (differences) between individuals in a species is caused by genes and the environment.
- The instructions for how an organism will develop are provided by genes.
- Each gene affects a specific characteristic.
- Genes are found in the nuclei of an organism's cells.
- Genes are sections of DNA molecules, which make up chromosomes.
- Chromosomes occur in pairs, except in the sex cells.
- One chromosome in a pair comes from the father and the other from the mother.
- Both chromosomes in a pair carry the same genes in the same place.
- A particular gene can occur in slightly different forms, called alleles.
- A pair of chromosomes can have the same or different alleles for a particular gene.
- If a dominant allele is present it will control the characteristic.
- A recessive allele will control the characteristic only if it is present on both chromosomes.
- The offspring of the same parents can be very different because they inherit different combinations of alleles.
- Cells make proteins by following the instructions provided by genes.
- All organisms use the same genetic code.
- Genetic modification involves the genes from one organism being artificially introduced into another.

- Bacteria and some plants and animals can reproduce asexually.
- Asexual reproduction involves the division of cells to produce new cells.
- Cells produced through asexual reproduction contain exactly the same genetic information.
- New individuals produced asexually are genetically identical to the parent. They are called clones.
- Any differences between these individuals and the parent are due only to the environment.
- The cells of multicellular organisms become specialised in the early stages of development.

Ideas about Science

Making Decisions

- Some questions cannot be answered by science.
- Ethical issues are concerned with what is morally right and wrong.
- Because people have different beliefs and experiences, there are often lots of different views on ethical issues.
- A common argument is that the 'right' decision is the one that leads to the best outcome for the majority of people involved.
- People may disagree with scientific procedures because they feel that they are unnatural or wrong.
- Some people think it is unfair that an individual can benefit from something which was only made possible because others took a risk, when they would not be prepared to take the same risk themselves.

- **HT** • There is often a significant difference between what *can* be done and what *should* be done.
- Different decisions on the same issue may be made in different social and economic contexts.

Module C1

Air pollutants can affect the environment and our health. However, there are options available for improving air quality in the future. This module looks at…

- the chemicals that make up air and the ones that are pollutants
- data about air pollution
- the chemical reactions that produce air pollutants
- what happens to pollutants in the atmosphere
- the steps that can be taken to improve air quality.

Pollutants in the Air

Pollutants are chemicals that can harm the environment and our health. They enter the atmosphere as a result of human activity, e.g. burning **fossil fuels**.

Pollutants that harm the environment can also harm humans indirectly. For example, acid rain makes the water in rivers and lakes too acidic for plants and animals to survive. This has a direct impact on our food chain and natural resources like trees.

Common pollutants and the problems they cause are listed in the table below.

Chemicals in the Air

The Earth is surrounded by a thin layer of gases called the **atmosphere**. It contains about 78% **nitrogen**, 21% **oxygen**, 1% **argon** and **other noble gases**. There are also small amounts of **water vapour**, **carbon dioxide**, and **other gases**. The amount of water vapour and polluting gases varies.

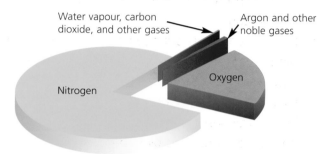

Water vapour, carbon dioxide, and other gases

Argon and other noble gases

Nitrogen

Oxygen

Measuring Pollutants

By measuring the **concentrations** of pollutants in the air it is possible to assess air quality. The units of measurement used are **ppb (parts per billion)** or **ppm (parts per million)**. For example, a sulfur dioxide concentration of 16ppb means that in every one billion (1 000 000 000) **molecules** of air, 16 will be sulfur dioxide molecules.

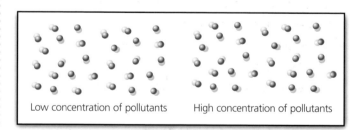

Low concentration of pollutants   High concentration of pollutants

Pollutant	Harmful to...	Why?
Carbon dioxide	Environment	Traps heat in the Earth's atmosphere (a greenhouse gas).
Nitrogen oxides	Environment Humans	Causes acid rain. Causes breathing problems and can make asthma worse.
Sulfur dioxide	Environment	Causes acid rain.
Particulates (small particles of solids, e.g. carbon)	Environment Humans	Makes buildings dirty. Can make asthma and other lung infections worse if inhaled.
Carbon monoxide	Humans	Displaces oxygen in the blood which can result in death.

Air Quality

Data about Pollution

Data is very important to scientists because it can be used to test a theory or explanation.

Example: One theory states that carbon monoxide (CO) is an example of a pollutant caused by human activity.

If this is true, carbon monoxide concentrations are likely to be higher in densely populated areas, e.g. cities.

The data below was collected on the same day using a carbon monoxide meter:

Location	Time	Carbon Monoxide Concentration (ppm)
City centre	9.00am	5.2
	10.00am	4.9
	11.00am	5.0
	12.00pm	2.6
	1.00pm	4.8
Country park	9.00am	0.2
	10.00am	0.1
	11.00am	0.1
	12.00pm	0.0
	1.00pm	0.1

Measurements like this can vary because...
- **variables** (factors that change), like volume of traffic and weather, affect concentrations
- all measuring **equipment** has a limited degree of accuracy
- the user's **skill** will affect the accuracy of the measurement.

Because the measurements vary, it is not possible to give a **true value** for the concentration of carbon monoxide in the air. However, the true value is likely to lie somewhere within the **range** of the collected data, i.e. between 4.8 and 5.2 in the city centre and between 0 and 0.2 in the country park.

The measurement of 2.6ppm has been excluded from the data range for the city centre, because it is an **outlier**. Outliers are measurements that stand out as being very different from the rest of the data.

They fall well outside the range of the other measurements and normally indicate some sort of error. You must be able to say why 2.6ppm is an outlier, e.g. the operator may have misread the scale. It is unlikely that the volume of traffic would have decreased at midday. In fact, you might expect it to increase as people leave their workplaces for lunch.

It is important that measurements are repeated. If you look at one measurement on its own, you cannot tell if it is reliable. However, if you look at lots of repeated measurements, any errors should stand out.

By calculating the **mean** (finding the average) of a set of repeated measurements, you can overcome small variations and get a **best estimate** of the true value.

$$\text{Mean} = \frac{\textbf{Sum of all values}}{\textbf{Number of values}} \quad \text{Do not use outliers in mean calculations!}$$

$$\text{City} = \frac{5.2 + 4.9 + 5.0 + 4.8}{4} = \textbf{5.0ppm}$$

$$\text{Country} = \frac{0.2 + 0.1 + 0.1 + 0.0 + 0.1}{5} = \textbf{0.1ppm}$$

The mean carbon monoxide concentration in the city centre is significantly higher than the mean carbon monoxide concentration in the country park. So, this data supports the theory that carbon monoxide is a pollutant caused by human activity.

In fact, about half of all carbon monoxide emissions in the UK are produced by road transport, with the rest coming from homes and other industries.

HT There is a **real difference** between the mean CO concentrations in the city centre and the park, because the difference between the mean values is a lot bigger than the range of each set of data. If the difference between the mean values had been smaller than the range there would have been no real difference. The result would have been insignificant and the data would not support the theory.

Chemicals

Elements are the 'building blocks' of *all* materials. There are over 100 elements and each one is made up of very tiny particles called **atoms**. All the atoms of a particular element are the **same** and are unique to that element.

Each element is represented by a different **chemical symbol**, e.g. C for carbon, O for oxygen and Fe for iron.

Atoms can join together to form bigger building blocks called **molecules**.

Compounds are formed when the atoms of **two or more different elements** are **chemically combined** to form molecules. The properties of a compound are very different to the properties of the individual elements it is made from.

Chemical symbols and numbers are used to write **formulae**. Formulae show…
- the different elements that make up a compound
- the number of atoms of each different element in one molecule.

Example

A water molecule, H_2O:

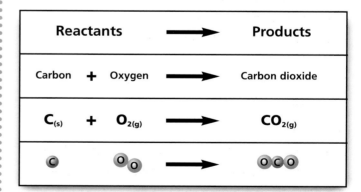

H_2O

Each molecule has…   two hydrogen atoms   one oxygen atom

Chemical Change

During a **chemical reaction** new substances are formed from old ones. This is because the atoms in the reactants (starting substances) are rearranged in some way:
- joined atoms may be separated
- separate atoms may be joined
- joined atoms may be separated and then joined again in different ways.

These chemical changes are **not** easily reversible.

You can show what happens during a chemical reaction by using a word equation. The **reactants** are on one side of the equation and the **products** (newly formed chemicals) are on the other.

| Reactants | ⟶ | Products |

Combustion

Combustion is a chemical reaction which occurs when fuels burn, releasing energy as heat. For combustion to take place, **oxygen** must be present.

Coal is a fossil fuel that consists mainly of carbon. The following equation shows what happens when coal is burned:

Reactants	⟶	Products
Carbon + Oxygen	⟶	Carbon dioxide
$C_{(s)}$ + $O_{2(g)}$	⟶	$CO_{2(g)}$
⊙ ⊙⊙	⟶	⊙⊙⊙

This equation tells us that one atom of carbon (solid) and one molecule of oxygen (gas) produces one molecule of carbon dioxide (gas).

No atoms are lost or produced during a chemical reaction. So, there will **always** be the same number of atoms on each side of the equation.

Air Quality

Burning Fossil Fuels

Many of the pollutants in the atmosphere are produced through the combustion of fossil fuels, e.g. in power stations, cars, aeroplanes etc.

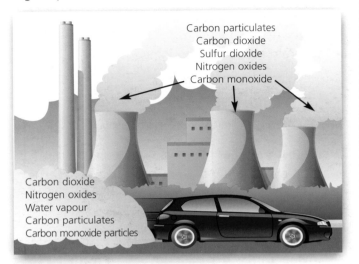

Carbon particulates
Carbon dioxide
Sulfur dioxide
Nitrogen oxides
Carbon monoxide

Carbon dioxide
Nitrogen oxides
Water vapour
Carbon particulates
Carbon monoxide particles

Complete Combustion

Fossil fuels such as petrol, diesel fuel, natural gas and fuel oil consist mainly of compounds called **hydrocarbons**. A hydrocarbon contains *only* **hydrogen** atoms and **carbon** atoms. So, when it is burned in air, **carbon dioxide** and **water** (hydrogen oxide) are produced (**complete combustion**). Remember, carbon dioxide is a pollutant!

Methane	+	Oxygen	→	Carbon dioxide	+	Water
$CH_{4(g)}$	+	$2O_{2(g)}$	→	$CO_{2(g)}$	+	$2H_2O_{(l)}$

Incomplete Combustion

If a fuel is burned and there is not enough oxygen in the air, **carbon particulates (C)** or **carbon monoxide (CO)** may be produced. This is called **incomplete combustion**.

Methane	+	Oxygen	→	Carbon	+	Water
$CH_{4(g)}$	+	$O_{2(g)}$	→	$C_{(s)}$	+	$2H_2O_{(l)}$

Methane	+	Oxygen	→	Carbon monoxide	+	Water
$2CH_{4(g)}$	+	$3O_{2(g)}$	→	$2CO_{(g)}$	+	$4H_2O_{(l)}$

Incomplete combustion occurs in car engines, so exhaust emissions contain carbon particulates and carbon monoxide as well as carbon dioxide.

Many samples of coal contain sulfur, so sulfur dioxide is released into the atmosphere when they are burnt.

Sulfur	+	Oxygen	→	Sulfur dioxide
$S_{(g)}$	+	$O_{2(g)}$	→	$SO_{2(g)}$

During the combustion of fuels, high temperatures (e.g. in a car engine or power station) can cause **nitrogen** in the atmosphere to react with **oxygen** and produce **nitrogen monoxide**.

Nitrogen	+	Oxygen	→	Nitrogen monoxide
$N_{2(g)}$	+	$O_{2(g)}$	→	$2NO_{(g)}$

Nitrogen monoxide is then **oxidised** to produce **nitrogen dioxide**.

Nitrogen monoxide	+	Oxygen	→	Nitrogen dioxide
$2NO_{(g)}$	+	$O_{2(g)}$	→	$2NO_{2(g)}$

When NO and NO_2 occur together they are called **NOx**.

What Happens to Pollutants?

Once pollutants have been released into the atmosphere they cannot just disappear, they have to go somewhere. This is when they can start causing **problems** for the environment.

Carbon particulates are deposited on surfaces such as stone buildings, making them dirty. The appearance of many beautiful old buildings has been changed due to this.

Some **carbon dioxide** is removed by natural processes; it is needed by plants for **photosynthesis** and some also **dissolves** in rain water and sea water, where it reacts with other chemicals in the water.

However, because we are producing too much carbon dioxide not all of it is used up naturally. The rest remains in the atmosphere, so each year the concentration of CO_2 in the atmosphere increases.

Because carbon dioxide is a **greenhouse gas** (it traps heat in the atmosphere) the rise in concentration is contributing to **global warming**, which is leading to **climate change**.

Sulfur dioxide and **nitrogen dioxide** dissolve in water to produce **acid rain**. Acid rain can damage trees, erode stonework, corrode metal and upset the pH balance of rivers and lakes. If water is too acidic, plants and animals will die and the whole food chain will be affected.

Carbon particulates are deposited

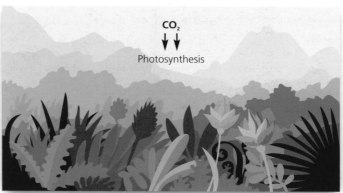

CO_2

Photosynthesis

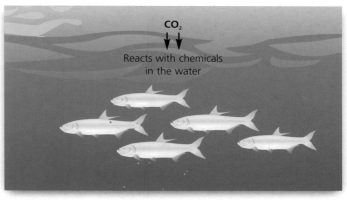

CO_2

Reacts with chemicals in the water

NO reacts with O_2 to produce NO_2

Sulfur dioxide can be blown by the wind and reacts with water to form acid rain

Nitrogen oxide (NO) and sulfur dioxide (SO_2) produced

Industry and power stations

Air Quality

Identifying Health Hazards

Because humans need to breathe in air to get oxygen, it is reasonable to assume that air quality will have some effect on the body.

To find out exactly how air quality affects us, scientists look for **correlations** (patterns) that might link a **factor** (e.g. a pollutant in the air) to an **outcome** (e.g. a respiratory complaint like asthma).

Example

We now know that **pollen** in the air causes **hay fever** in people who have a pollen **allergy**.

However, to reach this conclusion, scientists had to look at thousands of medical records. The data showed that most cases of hay fever occurred in the summer months when pollen counts were high.

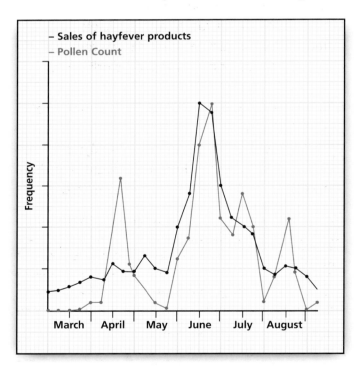

This correlation suggested that pollen **might** cause hay fever. However, it did not provide conclusive evidence because there were lots of other variables that could have influenced the outcome, e.g. temperature, humidity, other pollutants.

Further investigations, in the form of **skin tests**, were carried out to find out how pollen can affect health.

Pollen was collected in spore traps. The pollen was then stuck to the skin of volunteers using plasters.

In some volunteers the skin became red and inflamed indicating an **allergic reaction**. The results showed that people with a pollen allergy also suffered from hay fever. Those who did not have a pollen allergy did not get hay fever. This provided much stronger evidence of a link between pollen and hay fever.

HT When these findings were released, other scientists studied the data and repeated the skin test experiments. The fact that the tests always produced the same results proved that they were reliable.

Another condition that is linked to air quality is asthma. However, this example is more complicated. Studies of asthma have shown that when the concentration of NO_2 (nitrogen dioxide) increases in the air, more asthma attacks are triggered.

However, people still have asthma attacks when the levels of NO_2 are very low. This suggests that although NO_2 can increase the chance of an asthma attack occurring, it is not the primary **cause**.

There are many factors that can trigger an asthma attack. To fully understand what factors **cause** asthma and what factors may **aggravate** the condition, scientists need to study a large sample of people.

Improving Air Quality

Air pollution is everywhere. It affects everyone, so we all have a responsibility to reduce it.

Motor vehicles and power stations that burn fossil fuels are two major sources of atmospheric pollution, so we need to look at how emissions from these sources can be reduced.

Emissions from power stations can be reduced by...

- using less electricity so fewer fossil fuels need to be burned
- using a filter system to remove sulfur dioxide and particulates (carbon and ash) from flue gases before they leave a coal-burning power station's chimney
- removing toxic chemicals before they are burned, e.g. removing the sulfur from natural gas and fuel oil
- using alternative renewable sources of electricity, e.g. solar energy, wind energy and hydroelectric energy, to replace fossil fuels.

Solar Panels

Wind Turbines

Emissions from motor vehicles can be reduced by...

- buying a car with a modern engine that is more efficient and burns less fuel
- buying a hybrid car, which uses electric power in the city centre and can then switch to running on petrol for longer journeys
- using a low sulfur fuel (readily available) to reduce the amount of sulfur dioxide released
- converting the engine to run on biodiesel, a renewable fuel
- using public transport to reduce the number of vehicles on the road
- making sure cars are fitted with **catalytic converters**, which reduce the amount of carbon monoxide and nitrogen monoxide emitted.

The reactions that occur in a catalytic converter are:

Carbon monoxide	+	Oxygen	⟶	Carbon dioxide
$CO_{(g)}$	+	$O_{2(g)}$	⟶	$CO_{2(g)}$

Nitrogen monoxide	+	Carbon monoxide	⟶	Nitrogen	+	Carbon dioxide
$2NO_{(g)}$	+	$2CO_{(g)}$	⟶	$N_{2(g)}$	+	$2CO_{2(g)}$

The only way of reducing carbon dioxide emissions is to burn fewer fossil fuels.

Air Quality

Global Choices

In 1997 there was an international meeting about climate change in **Kyoto**, Japan. People from many nations agreed to reduce CO_2 emissions, and targets were set for individual countries. The governments of the countries are required to take appropriate measures to meet the targets.

National Choices

Here are just some of the rules and regulations that have been put in place by different countries to help meet their targets:

- setting legal limits for vehicle exhaust emissions, which are enforced by statutory MOT tests
- making catalytic converters compulsory on new vehicles
- using subsidies (grants) or reduced taxes to encourage power companies to use 'cleaner' fuels
- introducing a car tax system that encourages drivers to buy smaller cars with smaller engines
- encouraging investment in non-polluting renewable energy such as wind and solar energy.

These laws and regulations impact on many areas of science and industry. For example, when new cars are developed the technology used must meet all the legal requirements.

Some governments are concerned that steps taken to reduce carbon dioxide emissions will result in a decline in manufacturing and production, employment and the national economy.

Local Choices

Many local authorities are trying to encourage us to make environmentally friendly choices by providing...

- door step collections of paper, bottles, metals and plastics for recycling
- regular bus or train services
- electric trams (in some cities)
- congestion charges
- 'park and ride' schemes
- cycle paths and cycle parks.

Personal Choices

It is clear that the **choices** we make as **individuals** affect the amount of pollution in the air.

Using less energy in the home reduces the demand for energy from power stations, e.g. turning televisions off and not leaving them on standby.

Making sure your car is energy efficient and has a catalytic converter or choosing an alternative mode of transport, e.g. bicycle, cuts down on vehicle emissions.

Recycling materials like paper, bottles, metals and plastics helps to conserve natural resources, but also saves energy, e.g. it takes about 95% less energy to recycle an aluminium can than to make a new one.

There are other benefits to the 'green' options too. For example, walking and cycling instead of travelling by car help to keep us fit!

Science Explanations

Chemicals

- All materials are made from about 100 different chemicals called elements.
- Each element is represented by a different chemical symbol, e.g. Fe, H or Pb.
- An element is made up of very tiny particles called atoms.
- The atoms in each element are the same and are unique to that element.
- Atoms of different elements join together to make compounds.
- There are many different compounds because the atoms can join together in different ways.
- The properties of a compound are very different from the properties of the elements they are made from.
- In many compounds, different atoms of elements join together to form molecules.
- The composition of molecules can be shown using formulae, e.g. H_2O.

Chemical Change

- Chemical reactions produce new chemicals.
- In a chemical reaction, the atoms in the reactants are rearranged in some way.
  - Atoms that were joined together at the start may have separated.
  - Atoms that were separate at the start may have joined together.
  - Atoms that were joined at the start may have separated and then joined together in different ways.
- No atoms are destroyed or created in a chemical reaction.
- When hydrocarbon fuels burn, carbon and hydrogen atoms from the fuel combine with oxygen in the air to produce carbon dioxide and water.
- When fuels contain sulfur, they produce sulfur dioxide when burned.

Ideas about Science

Data and its Limitations

- Data is used to test scientific theories and explanations.
- Measurements do not always provide a true value.
- Repeated measurements of the same quantity often vary due to the skill of the scientist, the limitations of the equipment and external variables, e.g. fluctuations in air pollutants due to weather changes and emission levels.
- A best estimate of the true value can be found by calculating the mean of repeated measurements.
- If a measurement lies well outside the expected range of the true value it is probably incorrect and may be discarded.

Correlation and Cause

- A correlation (matching pattern) between a factor and an outcome suggests that one may cause or influence the other.
- Correlations have to be investigated further to eliminate any other factors that might influence the results.

 - A correlation between a factor and an outcome does not always mean that one causes the other.

The Scientific Community

- Scientists should be able to repeat experiments conducted by other scientists and get the same results.

 - If an experiment cannot be repeated, scientists may question its validity.

Science and Technology

- In many areas of scientific work, official regulations and laws control how science is used, e.g. legal limits on emissions restrict developments in car design and industry.

The Earth in the Universe

Scientific discoveries in the Solar System affect our understanding of the planet we live on and our place in the Universe. This module covers...
- what is known about Earth and space
- how the Earth's continents have moved and the consequences
- what is known about stars and galaxies
- how scientists develop explanations about Earth and space.

The Earth

Scientists once thought that the Earth was only 6000 years old. There was no way of testing this theory, so people believed it for a long time.

We now know that **rocks** provide evidence of how the Earth has changed and clues as to its age.

Erosion – the Earth's surface is made up of **layers** of rock, one on top of the other, with the oldest at the bottom. The layers are made of compacted **sediment**, which is produced by weathering and **erosion**. Erosion changes the surface of the planet over long periods of time.

Craters – the surface of the moon is covered with impact **craters** from collisions with meteors. However, the Earth, which is much larger, has had fewer meteor collisions (due to Earth's atmosphere) but craters have also been erased by erosion.

Mountain formation – if new **mountains** were not being formed the whole Earth would have been worn down to sea level by erosion.

Fossils – plants and animals trapped in layers of sedimentary rock have formed **fossils**, providing evidence of how life on Earth has changed over millions of years.

Folding – some rocks look as if they have been folded like plasticine. This would require a big force to be applied over a long period of time – further evidence that the Earth is very old.

Radioactive dating – all rocks are **radioactive**, but their radioactivity **decreases** over time. Radioactive dating measures radiation levels to find out how old they are.

Scientists estimate that the Earth is around **4500 million years old** – it has to be older than its oldest rocks – and when it was first formed it was completely **molten** (hot liquid) and would have taken a very long time to cool down.

> **HT** The oldest rocks that have been found on Earth are about **4000 million years old**.

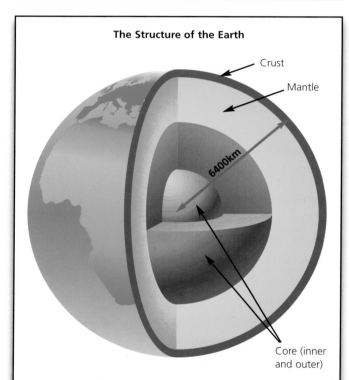

The Structure of the Earth

Crust

Mantle

6400km

Core (inner and outer)

Thin rocky crust
- Its thickness varies between 10km and 100km.
- Oceanic crust lies beneath the oceans.
- Continental crust forms continents.

The mantle
- Extends almost halfway to the centre.
- Has a higher density, and a different composition, than rock in the crust.
- Very hot, but under pressure.

The core
- Made of nickel and iron.
- Over half of the Earth's radius; has a liquid outer part and a solid inner part.
- The decay of radioactive elements inside the Earth releases energy, which keeps the interior of the Earth hot.

The Earth in the Universe

Continental Drift

Wegener (1880–1930) was a meteorologist who put forward a theory called **continental drift**.

He saw that the continents all fitted together like a jigsaw, with the mountain ranges and sedimentary rock patterns matching up almost perfectly. There were also fossils of the same land animals on different continents. So, he proposed that the different continents were once joined together, but had become separated and drifted apart.

How it once was

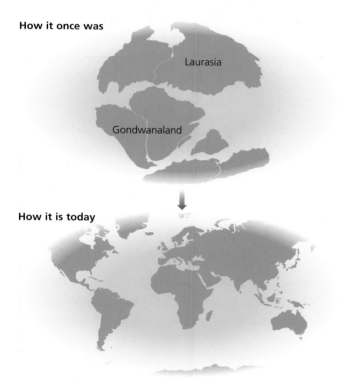

How it is today

Wegener also claimed that when two continents collided they forced each other upwards to make mountains.

Geologists at the time did not accept Wegener's theory because…

- he was not a geologist and was therefore considered to be an outsider
- it was a big idea but he was not able to provide much evidence
- the evidence could be explained more simply by a land bridge connecting the continents that has now sunk or been eroded
- the movement of the continents was not detectable.

Tectonic Plates

We now know that the Earth's crust is cracked into several large pieces called **tectonic plates.**

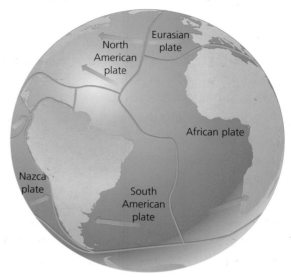

The plates float on the Earth's mantle because they are less dense. They can move apart, move towards each other or slide past each other. The lines where the plates meet are called **plate boundaries**. These are where **volcanoes**, **earthquakes** and **mountain formations** normally occur.

Earthquakes that occur near coastlines or at sea can often result in a **tsunami** (a tidal wave).

Geohazards

A **geohazard** is any natural hazard associated with the Earth, e.g. floods, landslides, hurricanes, earthquakes and volcanoes.

We get early warning signs before some geohazards, like hurricanes. The authorities can then take precautionary measures to protect people and property, for example…

- evacuating the area
- boarding up buildings or using sandbags
- putting emergency services on standby.

However, other geohazards strike with little or no warning so other measures to protect people are needed, e.g. buildings in earthquake zones are designed to withstand tremors, and the authorities will often refuse planning permission in areas prone to flooding.

The Earth in the Universe

Seafloor Spreading

Just below the Earth's crust, the mantle is fairly solid. Further down it is liquid and able to move. **Convection currents** in the mantle cause magma (molten rock) to rise to the surface. The force is strong enough to move the solid part of the mantle and the tectonic plates. When the magma reaches the surface, it hardens to form new areas of oceanic crust (seafloor), pushing the existing floor outwards.

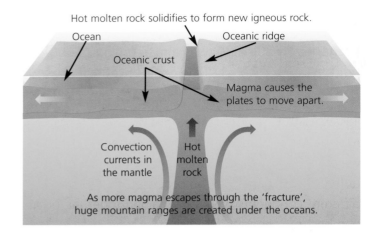

Hot molten rock solidifies to form new igneous rock.

Ocean

Oceanic ridge

Oceanic crust

Magma causes the plates to move apart.

Convection currents in the mantle

Hot molten rock

As more magma escapes through the 'fracture', huge mountain ranges are created under the oceans.

Plate Tectonics

New oceanic crust is continuously forming at the crest of an oceanic ridge and old rock is gradually pushed further outwards.

The Earth has a **magnetic field**, which changes polarity (reverses) every million years or so. Combined with the spreading of the seafloor, this produces stripes of rock of alternating polarity. Geologists can work out how quickly new crust is forming from the widths of the stripes. This occurs at **constructive plate boundaries** where the plates are moving apart.

When an oceanic plate and a continental plate collide, the denser oceanic plate is forced under the continental plate. This is called **subduction**. The oceanic plate then melts, and the molten rock can rise upwards to form **volcanoes**. The boundaries where this occurs are called **destructive plate boundaries**.

Mountain ranges form along plate boundaries as sedimentary rock is forced upwards by the pressure created in a collision.

Earthquakes occur most frequently at plate boundaries, when plates slide past each other or collide. Pressure builds up over many years due to the force of the plates pushing against each other. Eventually, the stored energy is released in a sudden upheaval of the crust and the energy spreads outwards in waves from the epicentre.

Plate movement plays a crucial role in the **rock cycle:**
- old rock is destroyed through subduction
- igneous rock is formed when magma reaches the surface
- plate collisions can produce very high temperatures and pressure, causing the rock to fold and changing sedimentary rock into metamorphic rock.

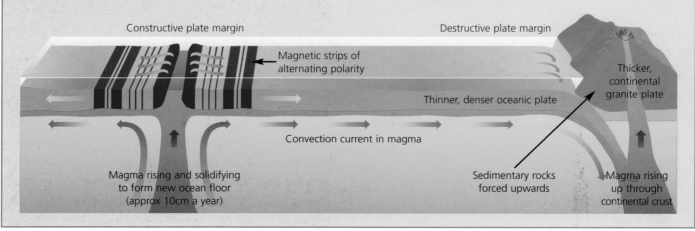

Constructive plate margin

Destructive plate margin

Magnetic strips of alternating polarity

Thicker, continental granite plate

Thinner, denser oceanic plate

Convection current in magma

Magma rising and solidifying to form new ocean floor (approx 10cm a year)

Sedimentary rocks forced upwards

Magma rising up through continental crust

The Earth in the Universe

The Solar System

HT The **Solar System** was formed over a very long period of time, about **5000 million years** ago.

1 The Solar System started as **clouds of dust and gas**, which were pulled together by the **force of gravity** (see diagram opposite).

2 This created intense heat. Eventually, **nuclear fusion** began to take place and a star was born: the **Sun**.

3 The remaining dust and gas formed **smaller masses**, which were attracted to the Sun.

The smaller masses in our Solar System are...

* **planets** – nine large masses that orbit (move around) the Sun
* **moons** – small masses that orbit the planets
* **asteroids** – small, rocky masses that orbit the Sun
* **comets** – small, icy masses that orbit the Sun.

Planets, moons and asteroids all move in **elliptical** (slightly squashed circular) orbits. Comets move in highly elliptical orbits (see diagram opposite). It takes our planet, Earth, **one year** to make a complete orbit around the Sun.

The Sun

The Sun's **energy** (heat and light) comes from **nuclear fusion**. **Hydrogen** atoms **fuse** (join) together to produce an atom with a larger mass, i.e. a new chemical element. During fusion, some of the energy trapped inside the hydrogen atoms is released.

All the **chemical elements** larger than helium were formed by nuclear fusion in **earlier stars**.

HT It is the **nuclei** of hydrogen atoms that fuse together during nuclear fusion.

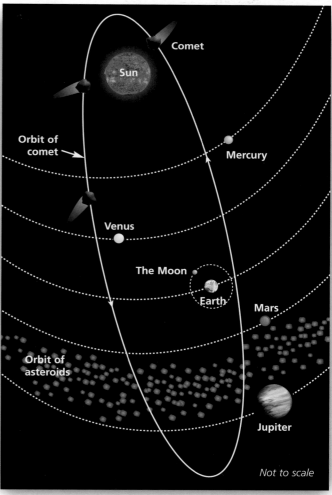

Not to scale

The Earth in the Universe

The Universe

At 5000 million years old, the Sun is only 500 million years older than the **Earth**. The **Universe** is much older than this: approximately **14 000 million years old** (almost three times older than the Sun).

Not to scale

Our planet – the Earth, 12 800km diameter

Our star – the Sun, 100 times wider than Earth

Our Sun

Our galaxy – the Milky Way, 100 000 light years across, containing at least 200 billion stars.

Our galaxy

The Universe – contains billions of galaxies, with vast distances between them.

The Speed of Light

Light travels at very **high** but **finite** (limited) **speeds**. This means that if the distance to an object is great enough, the time taken for light to get there can be **measured**.

> **HT** The speed of light is **300 000km/s** (around 1 million times faster than sound). So, light from Earth takes just over 1 second to reach the Moon (approximately 384 400km away).

Light from the Sun takes 8 minutes to reach the Earth. This means that when we look at the Sun, we are actually seeing what it looked like 8 minutes ago.

Vast distances in space are measured in **light years**. One light year is the **distance light travels in one year** (approx. 9500 billion km). The nearest galaxy to the Milky Way is 2.2 million light years away.

Measuring Distances in Space

Astronomers work out the distances to different **stars** using two different methods:

1 **Relative brightness**

In general, the dimmer a star is, the further away it is. However, stars can vary in brightness so we can never be 100% certain.

2 **Parallax**

If you hold out a finger at arms length and close each eye in turn, the finger appears to move. The closer the finger is to your face, the more it appears to move. Parallax uses this idea to work out distances.

As the Earth orbits the Sun, stars in the near distance appear to move against the background of very distant stars. The closer they are, the more they appear to move.

The position of a star is measured at 6-monthly intervals. These measurements can then be used to calculate its distance from Earth. However, the further away the star is, the more difficult and less accurate the measurement is.

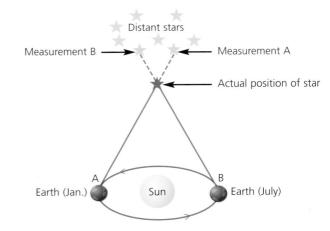

Distant stars

Measurement B → ← Measurement A

← Actual position of star

A | B

Earth (Jan.) | Sun | Earth (July)

Distant Stars

Because the stars are so far away, everything we know about them is worked out from the **radiation** they produce: **visible light** and other types of radiation including **ultraviolet** and **infrared**.

All our electric lights on Earth illuminate the night sky, so it is very difficult to see the stars sometimes. This is called **light pollution**. In 1990 the **Hubble Space Telescope** was launched. It orbits the Earth at a height of 600km, so it is not affected by light pollution.

The Life Cycle of a Star

All stars, including the Sun, have a finite life. Stars consist of hydrogen but, eventually, the supply of hydrogen runs out and the star swells up, becoming colder and colder to form a **red giant** or a **red super giant** depending on its size.

For medium-weight stars (like our Sun) see diagram ❶:

ⓐ the core of the red giant contracts to be surrounded by outer shells of gas which eventually drift away into space: this is a **planetary nebula.**

ⓑ as the core cools and contracts further it becomes a **white dwarf** with a density millions of times greater than any matter on Earth

ⓒ as the white dwarf cools it becomes a **black dwarf**.

For heavy-weight stars (at least 4 times the mass of our Sun) see diagram ❷:

ⓐ the red super giant rapidly shrinks and explodes releasing massive amounts of energy, dust and gas into space – a **supernova**.

ⓑ for stars up to 10 times the mass of our Sun the remnants of the supernova form a **neutron star**, formed only of neutrons. A cupful of this matter could have a mass greater than 15 000 million tonnes!

Our Sun will continue to shine for a further 5000 million years before becoming a red giant.

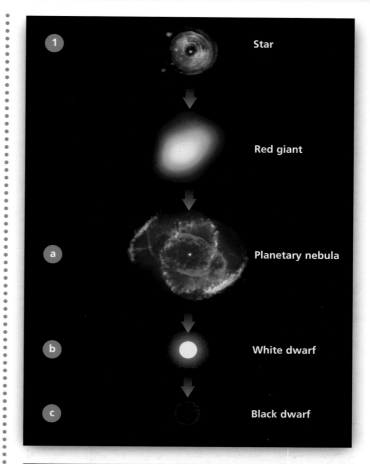

1
Star
Red giant
ⓐ Planetary nebula
ⓑ White dwarf
ⓒ Black dwarf

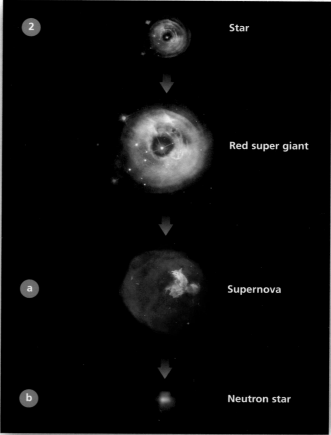

2
Star
Red super giant
ⓐ Supernova
ⓑ Neutron star

The Earth in the Universe

Other Galaxies

If a source of light is moving away from us, the **wavelengths** of the light are **longer** than they would be if the source was stationary.

The wavelengths of light from nearby **galaxies** are longer than scientists would expect. This means the **galaxies are moving away from us**.

HT In 1929 Erwin Hubble discovered that light from galaxies that were further away from us had even longer wavelengths. Therefore, they must be moving away from us faster. As a result, he developed **Hubble's Law**:

The speed at which galaxies are moving away from us is proportional to their distance from us (i.e. the faster a galaxy is moving, the further away it is).

If all the galaxies are moving away from us this must mean that space is **expanding** (getting bigger).

The Beginning

When scientists trace the paths of galaxies, they all appear to be moving away from the same point.

There have been many theories about how the Universe began. The one that best explains this evidence is the **Big Bang** theory, which says that the Universe started with a **huge explosion 14 000 million years ago**.

The End

The future depends on the amount of **mass** in the Universe. If there is not enough mass the Universe will keep expanding. If there is too much mass, gravity will grow powerful enough to pull everything back together and the Universe will collapse with a big crunch.

Measuring the amount of mass in the Universe is very difficult so its ultimate fate is hard to predict.

Aliens

In 1996 NASA announced that a Mars meteorite had been discovered, which appeared to contain a fossil of an ancient life form. After further study, other scientists offered different explanations for the patterns seen in the rock. The debate still rages with neither side able to convince the other.

If there are other life forms in the Universe they are likely to be on other planets or their moons. We know that at least some other stars have planets in orbit around them, because astronomers have been able to detect them.

At present there is no confirmed evidence of alien life, either past or present. However, there are thousands of millions of stars in our galaxy and thousands of millions of galaxies in the Universe. Many scientists think that with all these stars, even if only a small percentage have planets, it is unlikely that the only life forms in the Universe are on Earth.

BANG!

What Killed the Dinosaurs?

The dinosaurs became extinct around 65 million years ago along with nearly 75% of all species. This is scientific **data** (facts); there is evidence to prove it. One **explanation** for the extinction of the dinosaurs is that an asteroid collided with Earth.

A scientific explanation provides a **plausible reason** for **how** and **why** something happens. Scientists use their knowledge of how things work, and sometimes a bit of imagination, to explain how the data came about.

It is important to be able to tell whether statements relating to science are data (facts) or explanations (theories and ideas).

Explanation: An asteroid collided with Earth leading to the extinction of the dinosaurs.

The Facts

- Fossils show that the dinosaurs gradually died out over a few million years.
- Asteroids sometimes collide with planets.
- The probability of a large asteroid (several km in diameter) hitting the Earth is very small (the equivalent of once every 100 million years).
- If a large asteroid did collide with Earth, everything in the impact zone would be destroyed and there would be floods and fires in the surrounding areas.
- Large asteroids have collided with Earth in the past.
- The Chicxulub crater (in Mexico) provides evidence of an asteroid collision around 65 million years ago. Scientists estimate the energy released on impact was 10 000 times greater than all the world's nuclear weapons combined.
- A layer of iridium (a metallic element common in asteroids) is found all over the Earth.

The Explanations

- The layer of iridium around Earth could be the result of a collision with an asteroid.
- A big asteroid would have caused firestorms, shock waves, and possibly climate change. The dinosaurs would not have been able to survive.
- The asteroid collision could have released sulfur from the Earth's crust and caused extremely strong acid rain for weeks afterwards.
- The dust thrown into the air could have blocked out the Sun and caused plants to die, affecting the whole food chain.

A good scientific explanation will provide reasons for **all** of the data. However, many explain some of the facts but not *all* of them. The facts and explanations above could also be used to evaluate whether or not an asteroid could destroy the human race. Unlike the dinosaurs, humans have the means to be able to detect an asteroid moving towards Earth. However, that does not mean that we would be able to intercept or divert it, or have the means to survive its impact and effects.

The Earth in the Universe – Summary

Science Explanations

The Earth

- The Earth is a spherical planet moving around the Sun. It has a radius of approximately 6 400km.
- The Earth has four layers: inner core, outer core, mantle and crust.
- The crust is a thin layer of solid rock.
- The mantle is a thick layer of rock, which is very hot but under pressure. When pressure is reduced, it melts and the molten rock can rise and cause volcanoes.
- The inside of the Earth is kept hot by the energy released when the atoms of radioactive elements inside the Earth decay.
- Some changes in the Earth's surface take place over a very long time.
- The Earth's crust is being constantly eroded. It has not been eroded to sea level because new mountains are also being formed.
- Wegener suggested that the continents were once joined together, but became divided and drifted apart. He also proposed that mountains were formed when continents collided.
- Wegener's ideas about continental drift were initially rejected by geologists.
- The Earth's crust is split into tectonic plates, which are moved by convection currents in the mantle.
- The seafloor is spreading because new oceanic crust is being formed at boundaries, where two tectonic plates are moving apart.

> **HT** • Magnetic stripes on the ocean floor provide evidence for the sea floor spreading by about 10cm per year.

- The movement of tectonic plates is responsible for earthquakes, volcanoes and the creation of mountains.

The Solar System

- The Solar System is made up of the Sun, the planets that orbit the Sun, and their moons, asteroids and comets.

- The Earth takes one year to make a complete orbit around the Sun.
- The Sun is a star formed from clouds of dust and gas.

> **HT** • The Sun was formed about 5000 million years ago.

- The Sun will shine for another 5000 million years before becoming a red giant (which will destroy the Earth) and then becoming a black dwarf.
- The Solar System is part of the Milky Way galaxy, which contains billions of stars.

> **HT** • Energy in stars is released by hydrogen nuclei fusing together.

The Universe

- The Universe is vast and expanding; it is made up of billions of galaxies, which are all moving away from us. This suggests the Universe might have started in one place with a 'big bang'.
- We do not know if the Universe will keep expanding or if gravity will become strong enough to pull everything back inwards causing it to collapse.
- Astronomers have detected planets around other stars. Some believe that it is very likely that life exists elsewhere in the Universe.

Ideas about Science

Scientific Explanations

- A scientific explanation provides a plausible reason for how and why something happened. It can contain data (facts) and theories (ideas).
- A good scientific explanation accounts for all the known data.
- A good explanation for known data can also be used to make predictions.
- For some scientific questions, there is not a definite answer yet.
- It is important to be able to distinguish between data and theories.
- A theory needs reviewing and accepting by the scientific community before it is widely accepted.

Module B2

To stay healthy it is important to maintain a healthy lifestyle, practise good hygiene, and use medication when appropriate, e.g. to help prevent or treat illness. This module looks at...

- how our bodies resist infection
- what vaccines are and how they work
- what antibiotics are and why they can become less effective
- how new drugs are developed and tested
- what factors increase the risk of heart disease.

Infection

Infections are caused by harmful **microorganisms**. These microorganisms are divided into **three** groups:

Bacteria
e.g. bubonic plague, tuberculosis (TB), cystitis. Treated by antibiotics.

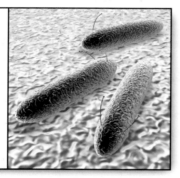

Fungi
e.g. athlete's foot, thrush, ringworm. Treated by anti-fungal medicine and antibiotics.

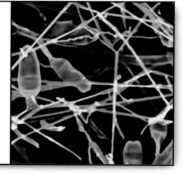

Viruses
e.g. H5N1 (Asian bird flu), common cold, HIV (Human Immunodeficiency Virus), measles, smallpox. Very difficult to treat.

The Body's Defence System

A huge number of microorganisms can be found on any surface and in the air that we breathe. However, the human body has a **defence system,** made up of **physical** and **chemical** barriers, which stops us getting ill all the time:

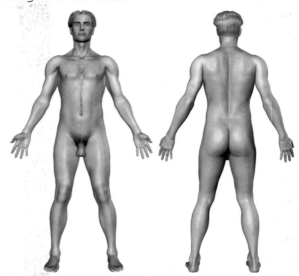

- The skin forms a physical barrier against invasion.
- Chemicals in sweat stop microorganisms from growing on the skin.
- Tears contain chemicals which kill microorganisms to stop them entering through the eye.
- The stomach produces hydrochloric acid which kills microorganisms that get into the food we eat.

The body provides the ideal conditions for microorganisms to thrive; it is warm with plenty of nutrients and moisture. Therefore, if harmful microorganisms do manage to get into the body they reproduce very rapidly – doubling in number every 20 minutes.

When the microorganisms first enter the body there are no symptoms of illness. Only when there is a significant amount of infection do the symptoms (e.g. nausea, pain or a rash) start to show.

These symptoms are caused by the microorganisms in one of two ways:
- by damaging infected cells in some way, e.g. bursting
- by producing harmful poisons (toxins).

Keeping Healthy

The Immune Response

If microorganisms do manage to break through the body's external defences, the **immune system** (the body's internal defence system) is activated to fight the invasion.

White blood cells play a major role in this response:

1. One type of white blood cell moves around the body in the bloodstream looking for microorganisms. When it finds some, it **engulfs** (flows around) them. It then **digests** the microorganism so that it is completely destroyed.

   This type of defence occurs when we get a cut and pus develops. The yellow liquid is mainly white blood cells which are full of digested microorganisms.

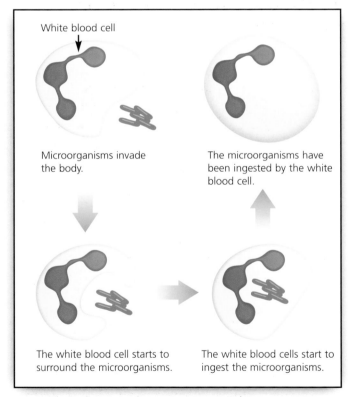

White blood cell

Microorganisms invade the body.

The microorganisms have been ingested by the white blood cell.

The white blood cell starts to surround the microorganisms.

The white blood cells start to ingest the microorganisms.

2. A different type of white blood cell makes special substances called **antibodies** (see diagram opposite) to combat infection. It takes time for white blood cells in the body to produce antibodies. This delay means that microorganisms continue to grow and cause illness (and sometimes death) before they are destroyed.

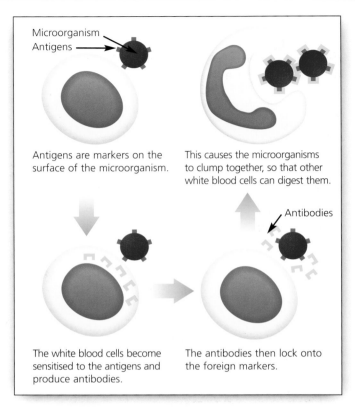

Microorganism
Antigens

Antigens are markers on the surface of the microorganism.

This causes the microorganisms to clump together, so that other white blood cells can digest them.

Antibodies

The white blood cells become sensitised to the antigens and produce antibodies.

The antibodies then lock onto the foreign markers.

Specialisation of Antibodies

Different diseases are caused by different microorganisms. Each microorganism has its own unique markers, called antigens, on its surface.

White blood cells produce antibodies specific to the type of marker they need to attack. This means, for example, that antibodies produced to fight tetanus will have no effect on TB or cholera because they have different markers.

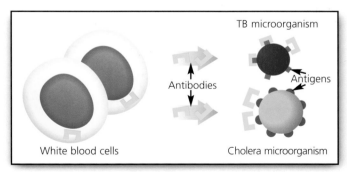

TB microorganism

Antibodies

Antigens

White blood cells

Cholera microorganism

When a person has had an infectious disease, the white blood cells 'remember' the antigens on the surface of the microorganism. As a result, they can produce antibodies quicker if they encounter the same microorganism again. This helps to protect the person against that particular disease and is called **natural immunity**.

Vaccination

Vaccination helps the body to develop long-term immunity against a disease, i.e. produce specific antibodies. So, if the microorganism that causes the disease enters the body, it will be destroyed before any damage is done:

1 Injection of vaccine

A weakened or dead strain of the disease-causing microorganism, which is incapable of multiplying, is injected.

2 Immune response triggered

Although the microorganism is modified, the antigens on its surface still cause the white blood cells to produce specific antibodies.

3 White blood cells remain in bloodstream

Long after the microorganism has been destroyed, white blood cells capable of attacking it remain in the bloodstream. If they come across the same antigen again, they can produce the right antibody much faster than they would if they had not encountered the microorganism before.

Side Effects

Vaccinations are never completely safe. They can produce **side effects** in some individuals. Most side effects are **minor**, e.g. a mild fever or rash, compared to the disease the vaccination is designed to prevent. However, some individuals are affected more than others.

More **extreme** side effects, e.g. encephalitis (inflammation of the brain) or convulsions, are **rare**.

With the controversial MMR (Measles, Mumps and Rubella) vaccination, the chances of getting encephalitis as a side effect are 1 in 1 000 000.

The risk of getting it from measles itself is between 1 in 200 and 1 in 5000 – much higher!

Mutating Viruses

Some vaccines are only effective for a limited period of time because viruses (e.g. influenza) can **mutate** (change) to produce a new **strain** (variety). As a result, new vaccines have to be developed regularly.

For example, flu vaccinations need to be renewed annually because every year a new strain of the virus will be around.

HT **HIV** (**Human Immunodeficiency Virus**), is a virus that attacks the immune system and which can lead to **AIDS** (**Acquired Immune Deficiency Syndrome**). Infected people often die from illnesses that a healthy person can fight off easily, e.g. the common cold.

HIV can be carried for many years without the infected person realising, because they have no symptoms. However, during this period the disease can accidentally be passed on to others.

It is extremely difficult to make an effective vaccine for HIV because…

- **it attacks the immune system** by infecting white blood cells, therefore, the defences that are needed in order to fight the virus do not work properly.
- **it mutates in the body** so even if a vaccine was developed, the virus can mutate rapidly and produce new strains which are not affected by the antibodies being produced by the body.

Keeping Healthy

Choices

Individuals have the right to say no to a vaccination. However, the more unvaccinated individuals there are in a population, the greater the chance of an outbreak of the disease and the faster it will spread.

> **HT** In order to prevent an epidemic of a disease like measles in a population, it is important that as many individuals as possible are vaccinated.
>
>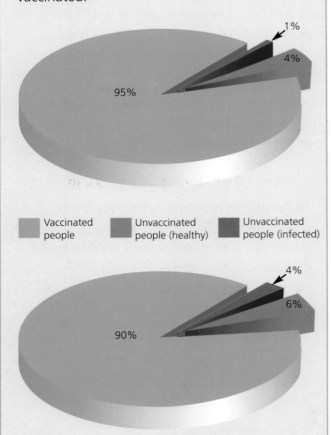
>
> - Vaccinated people
> - Unvaccinated people (healthy)
> - Unvaccinated people (infected)
>
> If over 95% of the population are vaccinated then the unvaccinated will be protected too. This is because the risk of coming into contact with an infected person is very small.
>
> If the percentage drops below 95%, unvaccinated individuals are more likely to come into contact with infected people and will pass the disease onto others who are unvaccinated (often members of the same family).

Vaccination Policy

Health authorities have to develop a policy (plan of action) for each different vaccination, which will benefit a majority of people. However, because people hold different views, there will always be some who disagree with the policy.

> **HT** Here are some of the key factors that must be considered when trying to decide on the best course of action:
> - **How high is the risk of infection?**
>   Some diseases like German measles are common in the UK, whilst others like typhoid are not such a risk.
> - **Who is most at risk?**
>   The very young, the elderly and people living in poverty (poor diet, etc.) might be at higher risk.
> - **Is the vaccination safe?**
>   The vaccination needs to have been fully tested to ensure it is effective and has no adverse effects.
> - **What is the cost?**
>   Can the Government afford to offer a free vaccine to everyone who needs one? Would the money be better spent elsewhere?
>
> There is always a difference between what **can** be done and what **should** be done (see p.11)
>
> For example, the government might have the ability to vaccinate everyone in the country, but it would be unacceptable to force everyone to have the vaccination. Here are just a few reasons why:
> - we live in a free society and have the right to choose for ourselves
> - vaccination may conflict with the religious/personal beliefs of an individual
> - some individuals may be more susceptible to the potential side effects than others.
>
> Different courses of action may be taken in different social and environmental contexts (see p.11).

Antibiotics

Bacteria and fungi can be killed by chemicals (or drugs) called **antibiotics**. Viruses cannot be killed by antibiotics. This is why doctors do not prescribe them for colds and flu.

Resistance to Antibiotics

Over a period of time, bacteria and fungi can become **resistant** to antibiotics.

> **HT** Random mutations can occur in the genes of microorganisms, which lead to new strains developing. Some of these new strains of bacteria and fungi are less affected by the antibiotics previously used so they are able to reproduce and pass on the resistance.

As more and more varieties of bacteria and fungi become resistant to certain types of antibiotics, there are fewer ways of defeating them.

There is growing concern that microorganisms which are resistant to *all* types of drugs will eventually develop. These are what the media dub **superbugs**.

In the UK, there are already diseases such as MRSA (Methicillin Resistant *Staphylococcus aureus*), drug-resistant TB and *Clostridium difficile* (an infection of the intestines), which have a high degree of drug resistance.

To help prevent resistance to antibiotics increasing…
* doctors should only prescribe them when completely necessary
* patients should always complete a course of antibiotics, even if they are feeling better.

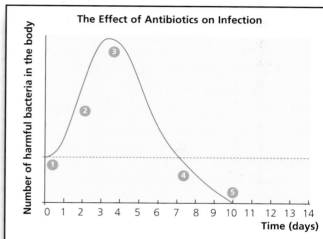

The Effect of Antibiotics on Infection

Number of harmful bacteria in the body vs *Time (days)*

1. Harmful bacteria enter the body (by food poisoning).
2. Bacteria multiply. Patient begins to feel unwell.
3. Patient visits doctor. Starts taking antibiotics.
4. Number of bacteria now lower than originally entered the body. Patient feels better (but bacteria not all dead).
5. All harmful bacteria now destroyed.

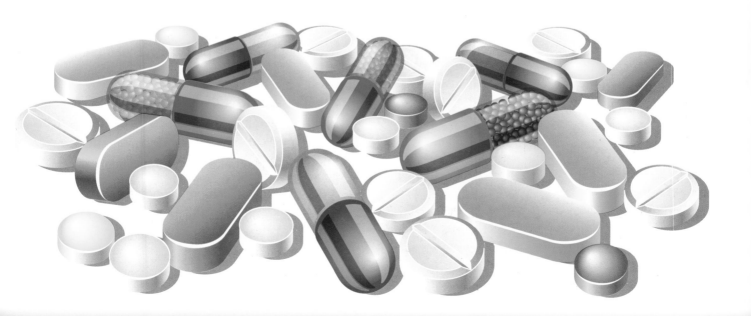

Keeping Healthy

Testing New Drugs

Scientists are always trying to develop new drugs to fight infection. Before they can be used, it is essential that the drugs are tested for **safety** and **effectiveness**. The methods used for testing drugs are often controversial.

Tests on different types of human cells grown in the laboratory

Advantages
- Shows if drugs are effective at fighting microorganisms.
- Shows if drugs will cause damage to cells.
- No people or animals are harmed.

Disadvantages
- Does not show effects of drugs on whole organism.
- Some people believe that growing human cells in this way is unnatural or wrong.

Tests on animals

Advantages
- Shows if drugs are effective within body conditions.
- Shows if drugs are safe for whole body.

Disadvantages
- Animals can suffer and die as a result of the tests.
- Animals might react differently to humans.

Following these initial tests (which can take years) **clinical trials** are carried out on **healthy volunteers** to test for **safety**, and on people with the **illness** to test for **safety** and **effectiveness**.

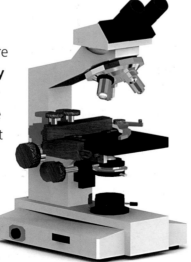

HT Clinical trials normally compare the effects of the new drugs to old ones. They have to be carefully planned to ensure the results are as accurate and reliable as possible. There are two types of trial:

1 Blind Trials
The patient does not know which drugs they are being given but the doctor does. If the patient knows what drug they had been given, they might give biased information. However, it is possible that the doctor's body language or reactions might give away information.

2 Double-blind Trials
Neither the patient nor the doctor knows which drug is being used. This means the results should be very accurate, removing bias. Although this is preferable, sometimes it is impossible to keep this information from the doctor, e.g. if the new drug has a different taste or different effects on the body.

Placebos (dummy drugs containing no medication) are occasionally used in clinical trials. However, this is not common practice because they create an **ethical** dilemma:

Trials involving placebos benefit society, because they help to establish whether a new drug is effective or not.

However, when doctors give sick patients a placebo they are offering them false hope; the patient hopes the pill will cure them, but the doctor knows it will not.

It is also difficult to disguise a placebo. If a new drug is expected to produce certain side effects and the patient does not display them, they may deduce that a placebo has been given.

For example, if a diuretic (increases urine production) is being tested, it would be easy to tell if the patient had been given the actual drug rather than a placebo.

The Heart

All living cells use oxygen to release energy from glucose. This process is called **respiration**.

The heart pumps blood around the body to provide the cells with oxygen (from the lungs) and nutrients, and take away waste materials.

The heart itself is made up of muscle cells. This means that it also needs a blood supply to keep functioning.

Arteries and Veins

The main blood vessels for transporting blood are **arteries** and **veins**. Their structure is related to their function.

Arteries carry blood away from the heart **towards** the organs. Substances from the blood cannot pass through the artery walls.

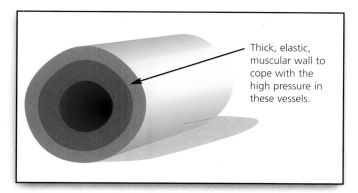

Thick, elastic, muscular wall to cope with the high pressure in these vessels.

Veins carry blood from the organs **back** to the heart. Substances cannot pass through the veins' walls.

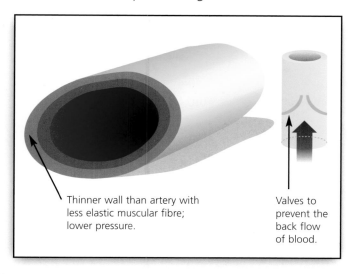

Thinner wall than artery with less elastic muscular fibre; lower pressure.

Valves to prevent the back flow of blood.

Heart Disease

Heart disease is a structural or functional abnormality of the heart, which can lead to a heart attack. It is usually caused by **lifestyle** and/or **genetic factors** not by infection (i.e. microorganisms). Elements of lifestyle that can lead to heart disease include…

- excessive alcohol intake
- poor diet
- smoking
- stress.

Fatty deposits can build up in the blood vessels supplying the heart. This means that blood flow is restricted and the muscle cells do not get the oxygen and nutrients that they need. This can cause a **heart attack**.

In the UK heart disease is much more common than in non-industrialised countries like Cambodia or Rwanda. This is probably because people in the UK are less active, e.g. they drive everywhere and use machines to do work, and the typical diet in the UK is high in salt and fats.

Reducing the Risk

There are precautions people can take to reduce the risk of heart disease.

- Exercise regularly (aim to raise the heart rate, without putting it under too much stress) e.g. 20 minutes of brisk walking every day.
- Do not smoke.
- Maintain a healthy body weight.
- Reduce salt intake, e.g. avoid salty foods and do not add salt to food.
- Monitor cholesterol levels (and use cholesterol reducing foods/drugs if necessary).

Keeping Healthy

Epidemiological Studies

If we can identify which lifestyle factors lead to heart disease, we can take action to prevent it.

Scientists try to identify these factors by examining the **incidence** (number of cases) and **distribution** of heart disease in large populations. These investigations are called **epidemiological studies**.

Correlation

Scientists look at a large **sample** (lots of individual cases, which represent a cross-section of the population) to see if there is a **correlation** (link) between a particular **factor** and an **outcome** like heart disease.

One correlation that has already been identified is between a high-fat diet (factor) and heart attacks (outcome). That is to say, a large proportion of people who suffered heart attacks had a high-fat diet.

It is important to remember that not all people who ate a fatty diet had a heart attack. This suggests that a fatty diet increases the chance of having a heart attack, but does not **always** lead to one.

HT A correlation between a factor and an outcome does not necessarily mean that the factor is a cause.

For example, a fictional study of obesity could uncover a positive correlation between the number of cans of diet cola an individual drinks and the number of kilograms they are overweight. This does not mean that diet cola **causes** people to be overweight. There is an alternative explanation – these people might drink diet cola **because** they are overweight!

Samples

Scientists have to look at a large sample to produce reliable results and establish what is typical and what is atypical (unusual) in a population.

An individual case might be atypical. However, without comparing it to lots of other cases, you would not know this and could easily reach the wrong conclusion.

For example, an individual who has smoked for most of his life might live to 98 without getting heart disease or lung cancer. If you looked at this case alone you might think that smoking helps you live longer!

To ensure a **fair test**, the individuals in a sample should be closely matched so that only the factor being investigated varies.

For example, if you were investigating the effect of smoking on life expectancy, the individuals in the sample would all need to have a similar diet and alcohol intake to ensure that those factors didn't affect the results.

HT Data gathered through investigations can be used to argue whether or not a particular factor increases the chance of an outcome and make predictions, for example...

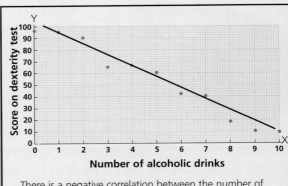

There is a negative correlation between the number of alcoholic drinks consumed and a person's dexterity (ability to move hands easily). As X increases, Y decreases. This means that given a value for X it is possible to make a prediction of the value of Y.

Even if a correlation between a factor and an outcome is supported by data, scientists might still reject it.

It is only likely to be accepted if scientists can find a plausible (likely) explanation for how that factor can bring about the outcome, based on what they already know about how the body works.

The Peer Review Process

Scientists follow procedures when conducting scientific research, like epidemiological studies, to ensure their findings are reliable:

1 Epidemiological Study

The scientist discovers a correlation between a factor and an outcome and makes a hypothesis, e.g. that factor X increases the chance of outcome Y.

2 Further Investigation

The scientist conducts further experiments / observational studies to gather data to test the hypothesis.

3 Reports Findings

The scientist writes a paper detailing the hypothesis, how the experiment was carried out, the results, and the conclusion (whether the data gathered supports the hypothesis or not).

4 Peer Review

The paper is sent out to the scientist's **peers** (other scientists who work in that field). They check and evaluate the paper to see if there are any faults or flaws. They may even repeat the experiments to see if they get the same results.

5 Findings Released

If it is decided that the research was carried out correctly and the conclusions are accurate, then the findings are published in a science journal or presented at a seminar.

6 Feedback

Once the findings have been released, all scientists can evaluate the evidence for themselves. The information might lead to further advances by other scientists. It could also be challenged – particularly if someone spots a problem that the initial reviewers (see stage 4) did not identify.

This process is very important. The more scientists that review and evaluate the findings, the more likely it is that errors and potential problems will be spotted, and the more reliable the results are likely to be.

Sometimes **preliminary results** (results that have not been fully reviewed by other scientists) are leaked to the press.

These results are not reliable and may turn out to be inaccurate or wrong. If the public are given inaccurate information like this it can cause problems, e.g. it can cause false hope or panic.

HT Unfortunately there are a small minority of scientists who make claims that are not true. They might do this to improve their reputation or to get more money / funding.

If a new scientific claim is reliable, other scientists should be able to conduct the same experiment and get the same results. If this is not possible, the scientific community **will not** trust the claim.

Likewise, if a scientist refuses to hand over evidence to support their claim (e.g. details of the experiments conducted and data collected) then their findings must be taken as being unreliable.

Monthly Scientist	April 2006

Faked Data, Misconduct and Lies

The work of a top Korean scientist came under the microscope this month, when an investigation revealed that his 'ground breaking' stem cell research was underpinned by a series of fabrications and lies.

The scandal highlights the need for an international regulatory body.

The role of such a body would be to preserve the integrity of the scientific community by implementing a compulsory review process to verify claims before they are released into the public domain…

Keeping Healthy – Summary

Science Explanations

Maintenance of Life

- All living cells respire.
- The heart pumps blood around the body, transporting oxygen from the lungs to the cells.
- The risk of heart disease is increased by poor diet, stress, smoking and excessive drinking of alcohol, and can be reduced by regular, moderate exercise.

The Germ Theory of Disease

- Many diseases are caused by microorganisms (e.g. bacteria, fungi and viruses) which are all around us.
- The body has natural barriers against microorganisms: the skin, chemicals in tears and sweat, and stomach acid.
- Conditions in the body mean that when microorganisms get in they reproduce very quickly.
- The symptoms of disease are caused by the microorganisms damaging cells or releasing toxins.
- The body's immune system fights against infections: some white blood cells engulf microorganisms and digest them, whilst others produce antibodies to destroy them.
- Different microorganisms require different antibodies.
- A vaccine is a modified microorganism (incapable of causing disease), which is injected into the body. The body produces antibodies, which means that it can produce them again rapidly if needed.

> **HT**
> - Vaccines are less effective against viruses because they can mutate and produce new strains.
> - It is difficult to develop a vaccine against HIV because the virus has a high mutation rate within the body.

- Microorganisms can cause illness, and even death, if the body does not destroy them quickly enough.
- Bacteria and fungi (not viruses) can be killed by chemicals called antibiotics.
- Over time bacteria and fungi can become resistant to antibiotics.

> **HT**
> - Mutations in the genes of bacteria and fungi can result in strains that are resistant to antibiotics.

- It is important to only use antibiotics when necessary and to complete the prescribed course.

Ideas about Science

Correlation and Cause

- There is a correlation between a factor and an outcome if…
  - the outcome always / often, or never / infrequently occurs when the factor is present
  - the outcome never / infrequently, or always / often occurs when the factor is not present.

> **HT**
> - A correlation between a factor and an outcome does not always mean that one causes the other.

The Scientific Community

- Scientific findings are only accepted once they have been checked and evaluated by other scientists.
- For scientists to accept a claim there needs to be a plausible explanation as to how a factor can bring about an outcome.
- If evidence is reliable other scientists should be able to repeat the experiment with similar results.

Decisions about Science

- Some scientific practices have ethical implications. There are often lots of different views and people disagree about what is right and what is wrong.
- When developing a policy concerning a scientific practice, like vaccination, it is important to look at what *can* be done and what *should* be done.
- Because different societies have different views and different resources available, they are likely to arrive at different decisions regarding scientific practices, like vaccination.

Material Choices

Module C2

We use materials for a variety of different functions everyday. Materials are often selected for a job because of the properties that they possess. This module looks at...
- the properties and structure of materials
- how polymers are created
- how the properties of materials can be altered
- the life cycle of a product
- how waste materials are disposed of.

Natural and Synthetic Materials

The materials that we use are chemicals, or mixtures of chemicals. Some materials can be made or obtained from living things e.g. cotton (plant), paper (wood), silk (a silk worm) or wool (sheep). Synthetic materials, produced by chemical synthesis, can be made as alternatives to these.

Crude Oil

When extracted, crude oil is a thick, black, sticky liquid. It contains mainly **hydrocarbons**, which are chain molecules containing only hydrogen and carbon atoms.

Different hydrocarbons have different boiling points, because their molecular chains are different lengths. This means that hydrocarbons can be separated by frictional distillation into different parts, or **fractions** (groups of hydrocarbons of similar lengths).

The petrochemical industry refines naturally-occurring crude oil to produce fuels, lubricants and raw materials for chemical synthesis. Only a small proportion of crude oil is used in chemical synthesis.

Properties of Materials

Different solid materials have different properties; they have different melting points and densities, and they can be strong or weak, rigid (stiff) or flexible, hard or soft.

The properties of a particular material mean that it will be better suited to some uses than others.

Examples

Unvulcanised Rubbers

Properties:	Uses:
• Low tensile strength	• Erasers
• Soft	• Rubber bands
• Flexible / elastic	

Vulcanised Rubbers

Properties:	Uses:
• High tensile strength	• Car tyres
• Hard	• Conveyor belts
• Flexible / elastic	• Shock absorbers

Plastic – Polythene

Properties:	Uses:
• Light	• Plastic bags
• Flexible	• Moulded containers
• Easily moulded	

Plastic – Polystyrene

Properties:	Uses:
• Light	• Meat trays
• Hard	• Egg cartons
• When foamed provides exceptional insulation properties	• Coffee cups
	• Protecting appliances and electronics
• Water resistant	

Synthetic Fibres – Nylon

Properties:	Uses
• Lightweight	• Clothing
• Tough	• Climbing ropes
• Waterproof	
• Blocks UV light	

Synthetic Fibres – Polyester

Properties:	Uses:
• Lightweight	• Clothing
• Waterproof	• Bottles
• Tough	

Material Choices

Properties of Materials (cont.)

The properties of the materials used will affect the durability and effectiveness of the end product, so manufacturers always test and assess them carefully beforehand.

Example

A supermarket needs to produce carrier bags. They can use either polythene or biodegradable plastic.

One factor which will determine their choice of material is strength, so they carry out the following investigation: a 2cm x 20cm strip of each type of plastic is placed in a clamp. (Each strip used must be exactly the same size to ensure a fair test). Weights are then gradually attached to the bottom of each strip to find the total weight it can support before breaking. The experiment is repeated a number of times to ensure the results are reliable.

Measurement	Maximum Weight (g)	
	Polythene	Biodegradable Plastic
1	2545g	1980g
2	2550g	1975g
3	2540g	1980g
4	5250g	1985g
5	2550g	1990g

When analysing data like this, look to see if any values stand out as being unusual, i.e. they look like **outliers** (see p.16). In the data collected for polythene the fourth measurement is an outlier. This is likely to have been caused by human error, e.g. the investigator writing the measurement down incorrectly, so it can be discounted.

The range (or span) of each set of data is from the lowest value to the highest value. The **true value** of the measured quantity is likely to lie within this range. Calculating the mean of a set of data helps to overcome any small variations and obtain a best estimate for the true value of the measured quantity (see p.16).

Mean Weight Polythene $= \dfrac{10185}{4}$

$= \mathbf{2546g}$

Mean Weight Biodegradable Plastic $= \dfrac{9910}{5}$

$= \mathbf{1982g}$

This data shows that polythene can hold more weight than the biodegradable plastic before breaking. In terms of strength, this makes it the most suitable material from which to make carrier bags. However, there are lots of other considerations the supermarket must take into account before making its final decision (see p.46).

Polymerisation

Polymerisation is an important chemical process in which small hydrocarbon molecules, called **monomers**, are joined together to make very long molecules called **polymers**.

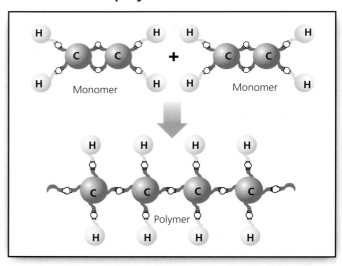

In this example the resulting long-chain molecule polymer is polyethene, often called polythene.

Remember that during a chemical reaction the number of atoms of each element in the products must be the same as in the reactants. Count the atoms!

Using Polymerisation

Polymerisation can be used to create a wide range of different materials which have different properties and therefore can be used for different purposes.

Many traditional (natural) materials have been replaced by polymers because of their superior properties.

Use	Traditional Material	Monomer	Polymer	Reason
Carrier bags	Paper	Ethene	Polyethene	Stronger; waterproof
Window frames	Wood	Chloroethene	Polychloroethene	Unreactive; does not rot

Molecular Structure of Materials

The properties of solid materials depend on how the particles they are made from are arranged and held together.

Natural rubber is very flexible. It consists of a tangled mass of long-chain molecules. Although the atoms in each molecule are held together by strong covalent bonds, there are very weak forces between the molecules so they can easily slide over one another allowing the material to stretch. Rubber has a low melting point as little energy is needed to separate the molecules.

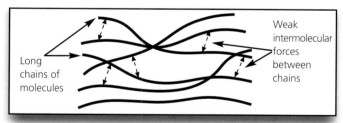

Long chains of molecules

Weak intermolecular forces between chains

Materials with strong forces between the molecules (covalent bonds or cross-linking bridges) have high melting points as lots of energy is needed to separate them. As the molecules cannot slide over one another, they are rigid and cannot be stretched.

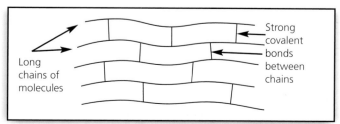

Long chains of molecules

Strong covalent bonds between chains

Modifications in Polymers

Modifications can produce changes to the properties of polymers. These modifications can include...

- **increasing the chain length** – longer molecules are stronger than shorter ones.
- **crosslinking** – crosslinks are formed by atoms bonding between the polymer molecules, so they are no longer able to move. This makes a harder material. An example of this is **vulcanisation**, when sulfur atoms form crosslinks between rubber molecules. Vulcanised rubber is used to make car tyres and conveyor belts.
- **plasticizers** – adding plasticizers makes a polymer softer and more flexible. A plasticizer is a small molecule which sits between the molecules and forces the chains further apart. The forces between the chains are therefore weaker and so the molecules can move more easily. Plasticized PVC is used to make children's toys, and un-plasticized PVC (uPVC) is used to make window frames.

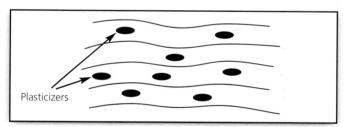

Plasticizers

HT A polymer can also be modified by packing the molecules more closely together to form a **crystalline polymer**. The intermolecular forces are slightly stronger so the polymer is stronger, more dense and has a slightly higher melting point.

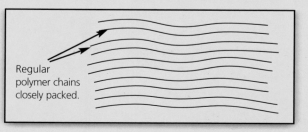

Regular polymer chains closely packed.

Material Choices

Life Cycle of a Product

Before a new product is produced, the manufacturing company must carry out a Life Cycle Assessment (LCA). The life cycle of a product, often known as Cradle to Grave, has three phases – **Manufacture, Use, and Disposal**. The LCA involves examining each of these three phases in detail, including the impact on the environment.

Each part of the life cycle of a product is carefully considered and assessed on the amount of energy and materials that will be used and how materials will be obtained and disposed of.

> (HT) The outcome of the LCA is dependent on several factors, including the use of the end product.

LCAs were introduced in the 1960s to encourage companies to reduce waste and be aware of environmental impact. New laws were put in place to protect the environment, cash incentives were offered to encourage recycling, and in 1996 a tax was introduced to discourage the use of landfill sites.

The purpose of an LCA is to ensure the most **sustainable** method is used, which means meeting the needs of today's society whilst allowing for the needs of future generations.

The diagram below shows what is being assessed in each stage of an LCA.

Manufacture (cradle)
Resources and energy needed to make the product. The environmental impact of making the product from the material.

▼

Use
Energy needed to use the product, e.g. fuel and electricity. Energy and chemicals needed to maintain the product. Environmental impact of using the product.

▼

Disposal (grave)
Energy needed to dispose of the product. Environmental impact of landfill, incineration and recycling.

Materials

Different materials can often be used to perform the same job. For example, disposable nappies are made from cellulose fibres, a super-absorbent polymer and fluff pulp whilst re-usable nappies are made from cloth. Disposable nappies may be more convenient but in a life cycle assessment which one is better for the environment?

The results of one study are shown below.

Impact per baby, per year	Re-usable nappies	Disposable nappies
Energy needed to produce product	2532MJ	8900MJ
Waste water	12.4m³	28m³
Raw materials used	29kg	569kg
Domestic solid waste produced	4kg	361kg

The evidence here shows that using re-usable nappies uses less energy, water and natural resources, whilst also producing less waste. This would suggest that people should be encouraged to use re-usable nappies.

Since 2003 it has been Government policy to encourage parents to reduce the number of disposable nappies they use.

Functions

The same material can be used to perform different jobs, for example, Teflon® (polytetrafluoroethene) was accidentally discovered in 1938 by Roy Plunkett. It is **chemically inert** and temperature resistant and there is also little impact of environmental damage when disposed of in landfill sites.
Teflon can be used in…

- gaskets and valves
- atomic bombs
- non-stick saucepans
- dentures.

Waste Management

To manage the waste that arises from our use of products we need to assess the environmental impact of each method of disposal, as well as the overall cost and loss of raw materials. There are three main methods for disposing of waste products and materials:

1 Use of Landfill Sites

Many materials such as plastics are non-biodegradable. Microorganisms have no effect on them so they will not decompose or rot away. The use of landfill sites for these non-biodegradable products can result in the waste of valuable resources, because nothing is being reused or returned to the environment.

Some materials that do slowly degrade produce landfill gas (methane). Methane can be used to generate electricity, but if too much gas builds up underground it can cause an explosion.

If landfill sites are properly lined, they cause no harm to the environment and eventually the land can be reclaimed, e.g. for parks. However, in the past toxic waste has escaped when the site has been poorly engineered. Landfill is also taxed.

2 Incineration

Incineration, or burning materials, produces air pollution. The production of carbon dioxide contributes to the Greenhouse Effect, which results in global warming.

Some plastics produce toxic fumes when they are burned, e.g. the burning of poly(chloroethene), PVC,

produces hydrogen chloride gas. Incineration again wastes valuable resources.

Newly built incinerators burn waste material at high temperatures to avoid the production of many harmful gases. The heat released from an incinerator could be used to produce steam to drive an electricity generator; this can save on the burning of fossil fuels to produce electricity. Apart from any gases, the only other waste product produced will be the ash.

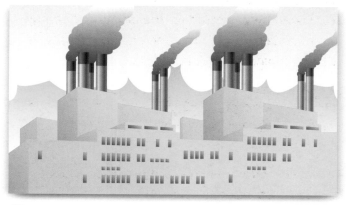

3 Recycling

Recycling a product means that no new material needs to be made. This conserves our raw materials, money and energy. People should be encouraged to re-use products such as polyethene carrier bags and glass bottles.

However, it is very expensive to recycle some materials, e.g. plastics need to be sorted into their different types before they can be recycled. This is often done by hand and is very time consuming. Every time polyethene is recycled its long molecules tend to get torn, so it becomes weaker, and the quality of the product is reduced.

Material Choices

Example LCA: A Polypropylene Food Box

Stage of Life Cycle	Assessment questions – Energy requirements	Assessment questions – What is the environmental impact of each stage?
Manufacture	How much energy would be needed… • to drill the oil? • to distil the oil? • for polymerisation? • to mould the box? • to transport the materials between stages?	• How much oil will need to be taken from natural reserves? • What is the risk of oil spillage during transportation? • What method of transportation is required and how does it affect the environment? • What pollutants are produced during manufacture and transportation?
Use	How much energy would be required… • to fill the boxes with food? • to store the boxes, e.g. in a fridge or freezer? • to transport the boxes between the factory, shop and consumer's home?	• How will the product be transported between the factory, shop and consumer's home and how does this affect the environment? • What pollutants are produced during filling and transportation?
Disposal	How much energy would be used or recovered if the box was… • reused? • recycled? • incinerated? • thrown away?	• Would incineration produce pollutants / toxic gases? • How much energy could be reclaimed through incineration? • How much energy is needed to recycle the boxes and what is the cost? • What is the value of materials and energy wasted if the box is thrown away? • How much landfill would it generate?

Although the government regulates industrial processes, e.g. there is a limit on emissions of pollutants, the manufacturers still have choices to make.

They must evaluate the answers to all of these questions and compare LCAs for producing the same product but using different materials. In some cases the most environmentally friendly materials and methods may be too expensive so a different method will be used.

The examples above are all questions that can be answered using scientific models and investigations. However, there are some answers that cannot be found in this way. For example, the manufacturer needs to decide whether the amount of energy and resources used, and the impact on the environment, is justified to produce a convenience product.

Material Choices – Summary

Science Explanations

Materials and Properties

- All materials that we use are chemicals or mixtures of chemicals.
- Natural materials are found in the world around us, in non-living things such as the Earth's crust or living things such as plants and animals.
- Synthetic materials are alternatives to natural materials.
- A material may be chosen for its particular properties such as melting point; strength (tension and compression); stiffness; hardness; density.
- The properties of solid materials depend on how the molecules are arranged.
- Materials which have strong forces between the molecules require more energy to separate them and they therefore have high melting points.
- The properties of a material can be modified to increase its usefulness, e.g. making it stronger or more flexible.
- Modifications can include increasing chain length; cross-linking; the use of plasticizers.

HT
- Increased **crystallinity** can be used to modify a polymer.

- Crude oil consists mainly of hydrocarbons.
- A hydrocarbon is a chain molecule containing only hydrogen and carbon atoms.
- In hydrocarbons the length of the chain determines the boiling points.
- Small molecules that can be joined together are called monomers.
- Monomers can be joined together to form long-chains of molecules called polymers. This process is called polymerisation.

Life Cycle

- The life cycle of a product has three phrases – manufacture, use and disposal.
- Different materials can be used for the same job.
- The same material can be used for different jobs.

- There is an environmental impact associated with all the methods of disposing of waste – landfill sites, incineration and recycling.

Ideas about Science

Data and its Limitations

- Data is used to gain a better understanding of the properties of materials.
- Measurements do not provide a true value.
- Repeated measurements of the same quantity often vary due to the skill of the scientist, the limitations of the equipment, and external variables, e.g. different batches of a polymer made at different times.
- A best estimate of the true value can be found by calculating the mean of repeated measurements.
- If a measurement lies well outside the expected range of a true value it is probably incorrect and may be discarded.

Correlation and Cause

- It is important to control all the factors that are likely to affect the outcome, i.e. to carry out a fair test. This allows reliable and meaningful measurements to be taken.

Science and Technology

- When a new product is developed, by Law, a Life Cycle Assessment must be carried out.
- The environmental impact of a product, from manufacture to disposal, needs to be assessed.
- The beneficial effects of the product need to be weighed against economic and environmental costs.
- Sustainable ways of manufacturing products are encouraged to conserve our natural resources for future generations.

Radiation and Life

Radiation is all around us and, whilst there are some dangers and hazards, certain radiations are essential to life on this planet. This module covers...

- the electromagnetic spectrum
- how radiation is transmitted
- ionising radiation and any harmful effects
- what happens to sunlight entering the Earth's atmosphere
- the carbon cycle and evidence of global warming.

The Electromagnetic Spectrum

The electromagnetic spectrum is a family of seven **radiations,** including visible light.

A beam of electromagnetic radiation contains 'packets' of energy called **photons**. Different radiations contain photons that carry different amounts of energy.

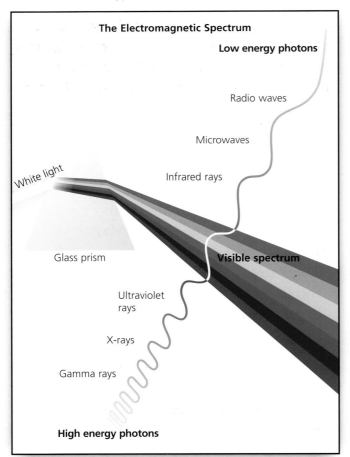

The Electromagnetic Spectrum

Low energy photons

Radio waves

Microwaves

White light

Infrared rays

Glass prism

Visible spectrum

Ultraviolet rays

X-rays

Gamma rays

High energy photons

Transmitting Radiation

A general model of radiation describes how energy travels from a source which emits radiation, to a detector which absorbs radiation.

Examples

Emitter	How waves travel	Detector
TV transmitter	Radio waves	TV aerial
Mobile phone mast	Microwaves	Mobile phones
The Sun	Light	The eye
Remote control	Infrared waves	Television
Some stars (e.g. supernova)	Gamma rays	Gamma-ray telescope
X-ray machine	X-rays	Photographic plate

On the journey from emitter to detector the radiation can be transmitted, reflected or absorbed by materials. For example, on a cloudy day, energy from the Sun is absorbed and reflected by the clouds, and the amount of light received at the ground is less than it would be on a sunny day.

Intensity and Heat

The **intensity** of electromagnetic radiation is the **energy** arriving at a surface **per second**.

The intensity depends on the number of photons delivered per second and the amount of energy each individual packet contains, i.e. the photon energy.

The intensity of a beam of radiation decreases with distance, so the further away from a source you are, the lower the intensity.

HT This decrease in intensity is due to three factors:
- The photons spread out as they travel so the energy is more spread out.
- Some of the photons are absorbed by particles in the substances they pass through.
- Some of the photons are reflected and scattered by other particles.

These effects combine to reduce the number of photons arriving per second at a detector, resulting in a lower measured intensity.

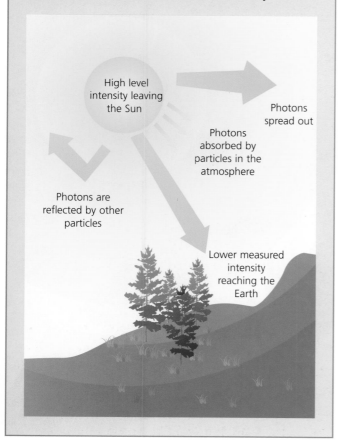

High level intensity leaving the Sun

Photons spread out

Photons absorbed by particles in the atmosphere

Photons are reflected by other particles

Lower measured intensity reaching the Earth

When a material absorbs radiation, heat is created; the amount of heat depends on its intensity.

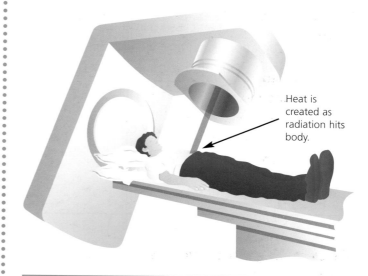

Heat is created as radiation hits body.

HT The amount of heat created also depends on the duration of exposure.

Ionising Radiation

Ionising radiation (electromagnetic radiations with a high photon energy) is able to break molecules into bits called **ions**. Ultraviolet radiation, X-rays and gamma rays are all examples of ionising radiations.

UV radiation

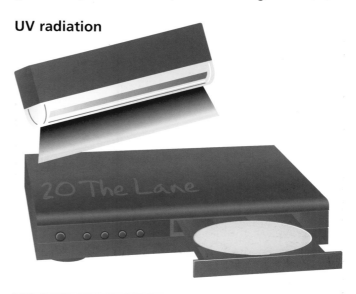

20 The Lane

HT Ions are very reactive and can easily take part in other chemical reactions.

Radiation and Life

Cell Damage

When living cells absorb radiation, damage can occur in different ways:

- The heating effect can cause damage e.g. sunburn.
- Ionising radiation, such as UV radiation, can damage cells, causing ageing of the skin.
- Ionising radiation can cause mutations in the nucleus of a cell, which can lead to cancer.
- Different amounts of exposure can cause different effects, e.g. high intensity ionising radiation can destroy cells, leading to radiation poisoning.

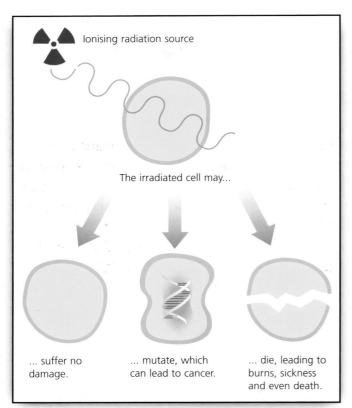

Ionising radiation source

The irradiated cell may...

... suffer no damage.

... mutate, which can lead to cancer.

... die, leading to burns, sickness and even death.

Microwaves can be used to heat materials containing water particles which the microwaves cause to vibrate.

There may be a health risk from the low intensity microwaves of mobile phone handsets and masts but this is disputed. A study in 2005 found no link from short-term use but other studies have found some correlation between mobile phone masts and health problems. Further studies are underway to look in more detail at mobile phone masts and the long-term effects of mobile phone use.

Radiation Protection

Microwave ovens have a metal case and a wire screen in the door – this absorbs the microwaves and protects users by preventing too much radiation from escaping.

Other physical barriers are used to protect people from ionising radiation:

- X-ray technicians use lead screens to prevent exposure.
- Sunscreens and clothing can absorb most of the ultraviolet radiation from the Sun which helps to prevent skin cancer.
- Nuclear reactors are encased in thick lead and concrete to prevent radiation escaping into the environment.
- People going into an area that they know contains high levels of radiation must wear a radiation suit, which is made from materials that act as a shield against the radiation.

The Sun's Energy

Light from the Sun is able to pass through the Earth's atmosphere. This radiation...

• warms the Earth's surface. The temperature is often high enough for water to be liquid.

• is used by plants as the energy source for photosynthesis.

Photosynthesis counteracts the effects of respiration – it removes carbon dioxide from, and adds oxygen to, the atmosphere.

The Ozone Layer

The ozone layer is a thin layer of gas in the Earth's upper atmosphere. This layer of gas absorbs some of the ultraviolet radiation from the Sun before it can reach Earth.

Without the ozone layer, the amount of ultraviolet radiation reaching Earth would be very harmful to living organisms, especially animals, due to cell damage. (see p.52).

> **HT** The energy from the ultraviolet radiation causes chemical changes in the upper atmosphere when it is absorbed by the ozone layer, but these changes are reversible.

The Greenhouse Effect

The Earth emits electromagnetic radiation into space but there are gases in the atmosphere which absorb some of this radiation. This keeps the Earth warmer than it would otherwise be, and is known as the **Greenhouse Effect**. Carbon dioxide is a greenhouse gas and makes up a small amount of the Earth's atmosphere, about 0.035%.

> **HT** Other greenhouse gases include water vapour and trace amounts of methane.

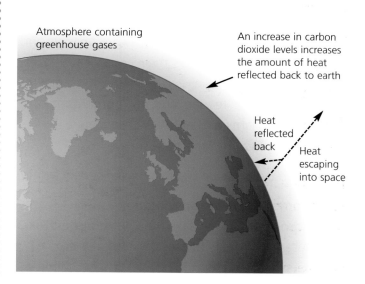

Atmosphere containing greenhouse gases

An increase in carbon dioxide levels increases the amount of heat reflected back to earth

Heat reflected back

Heat escaping into space

Radiation and Life

The Carbon Cycle

The carbon cycle is an example of a balanced system.

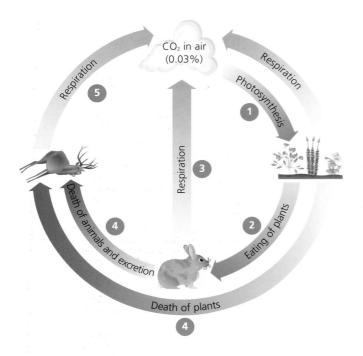

1. CO_2 is removed from the atmosphere by green plants to produce glucose by photosynthesis. Some is returned to the atmosphere by the plants during respiration.
2. The carbon obtained by photosynthesis is used to make carbohydrates, fats and proteins in plants. When the plants are eaten by animals this carbon becomes carbohydrates, fats and proteins in animals.
3. Animals respire releasing CO_2 into the atmosphere.
4. When plants and animals die, other animals and microorganisms feed on their bodies causing them to break down.
5. As the detritus feeders and microorganisms eat the dead plants and animals, they respire releasing CO_2 into the atmosphere.

The carbon cycle can be used to explain several points:

- The amount of **carbon dioxide** in the atmosphere had remained roughly constant for thousands of years because the levels were constantly being recycled by plants and animals.
- The importance of **decomposers,** which are microorganisms that break down dead material and release carbon dioxide back into the atmosphere.
- The amount of carbon dioxide in the atmosphere has been steadily increasing over the last 200 years, largely due to human activity such as burning fossil fuels and deforestestation.
- **Fossil fuels** contain carbon that was removed from the atmosphere millions of years ago, and has been 'locked up' ever since. Burning fossil fuels for energy releases this carbon into the atmosphere.
- **Burning forests (deforestation)** to clear land not only releases the carbon they contain but also reduces the number of plants removing carbon dioxide from the atmosphere.

Global Warming

The increase of greenhouse gases in the Earth's atmosphere, especially carbon dioxide, means that the amount of absorbed radiation from the Sun also increases. This increases the temperature on Earth, an effect known as global warming. As the Earth becomes hotter, there are some potential results:

1. **Climate change** – it may become impossible to grow some food crops in certain areas.
2. **Extreme weather conditions**, e.g. floods, droughts, hurricanes.
3. **Rising sea levels** – the melting ice caps and higher ocean temperatures may cause sea levels to rise which could cause flooding of low-lying land. Some pacific islands have already been abandoned.

Causes of Global Warming

Climatologists collect data about how the Earth's temperature has changed over the years. The data collected is used with climate models to look for patterns. These computer models show that one of the main factors causing global warming is the rise in atmospheric carbon dioxide and other greenhouse gases, providing evidence that human activities are causing global warming.

Risk and Benefit

Assessing Risk

With almost all new discoveries and advances there is a potential for a risk either to the environment or people's health. Because of the damage that radiation can cause to living cells, no scientific or technological advances in this field are likely to be without risk.

For example, whilst X-rays allow doctors to make a much more accurate diagnosis, exposure times have to be carefully controlled to prevent cell damage. And whilst radiation can be used to destroy cancerous cells in the body, it can have the opposite effect if it comes into contact with healthy cells. Therefore, it is important to be able to evaluate the risks and benefits carefully.

Opposite is an extract from an article about mobile phones. Until scientists are able to prove or disprove a correlation between mobile phones and cancer, individuals need to make their own decisions by weighing up the benefits and potential risks, and looking at whether the risks can be reduced in any way.

Benefits
• Easy convenient method of communication, especially in a vulnerable situation, e.g. when car breaks down, alone at night, feel threatened. • Easy way to keep in contact when away from home.

Risks
• Some studies have linked mobile phones to brain tumours. • Studies are still being carried out and the long-term effects of using mobile phones are not known.

Risk Reduction
• Limit usage to emergency situations and text messaging. • Use a hands-free kit. • Avoid using phone when the signal is low (phone is having to work harder).

Example

Phone study looks at radiation risk

A number of studies have been carried out by scientists in Scandinavian countries to try to establish whether the radiation from mobile phones is a health risk, and can increase the risk of cancer.[1]

Most found that the rates of cancer in mobile phone users were no higher than in other groups.[2]

Although it was found that mobile phones can raise the temperature of the brain by approximately 0.1°C, the temperature of the brain naturally fluctuates throughout the day by amounts greater than this, so there is no reason to think that mobile phones cause damage or increase the risk of cancer.

However, brain cancer is fairly uncommon, so it can be difficult to find enough individuals to form a reliable sample group to test this theory.[3] As a result, scientists from different countries are working together to produce an international survey.

Results so far show that even people who have regularly used mobile phones for over 10 years show no increased risks of the two most common types of brain cancer. Although the risk of them getting acoustic neuroma, a benign tumour affecting the nerve between the ear and brain, did appear to be increased.[4]

FOOTNOTES

HT **1** They are looking for a **correlation** (link) between the radiation from mobile phones (factor) and an increased risk of cancer (outcome).

2 No correlation is found.

3 Individual cases and small sample groups do not provide convincing evidence, because scientists cannot know if they are demonstrating unusual or normal behaviour, i.e. whether they are representative of the population.

HT **4** This suggests that the radiation from mobile phones (factor) might increase the chance of a user getting acoustic neuroma (outcome), but does not always lead to it (if this was the case all users would have the tumour).

Radiation and Life

Risk and Benefit (cont.)

HT Because mobile phones are a relatively new technology, scientists cannot know the long-term effects of using them. Some believe it is better therefore to take **precautionary measures**, e.g. limiting usage, especially for young people whose bodies are still developing and might be more vulnerable to the effects.

Weighing the Risks

It is impossible for any activity to be completely safe; there will always be a potential for accident or harm. However, in weighing up a risk it is important to consider what the chance of the outcome occurring is, and what the consequences would be if it did happen. For example, in the case of using mobile phones, although the risk seems low, the outcome could be a terminal disease.

Example

It is well documented that scientists have produced reliable evidence to support the idea that prolonged exposure to ultraviolet light considerably increases the risk of skin cancer.

This means that by taking measures to reduce exposure to UV rays, individuals can reduce the risk of skin cancer significantly. However, many people still sunbathe and use sun beds. Some reasons for this could be...

- a certain amount of sunlight is needed for good health; it is a source of vitamin D
- sunlight can help prevent SAD (seasonal affective disorder) and skin conditions such as eczema
- people think a tan looks healthy / more attractive (an idea promoted by the media)
- individuals believe it will never happen to them.

HT **Actual risk** is a scientific measure of the dangers of something. **Perceived risk** is how dangerous people think it is. Often these values can be vastly different. Factors that can affect perceived risk include…

- media coverage
- personal bias
- social influence, e.g., the opinions of family and peers.

With regard to radiation sources, the **ALARA** (as low as reasonably achievable) principle is used as a guideline for risk management.

It states that measures should be taken to make the risks as small as possible, whilst still providing the benefits and taking into account all social, economic and practical implications.

For example, this is used in radiology units at hospitals, to ensure that staff are protected from exposure whilst administering effective treatments to patients, and to control the dose of radiation given in each treatment.

Radiation and Life – Summary

Science Explanations

The Electromagnetic Spectrum

- The electromagnetic spectrum is a family of radiations: radio, microwave, infrared, visible light, ultraviolet, X-ray, gamma.
- The spectrum of visible light extends in both directions (towards infrared and ultraviolet).

Radiation

- A photon is a packet of energy.
- Information can be transmitted as electromagnetic radiation. A transmitted signal can be affected by materials in the way.
- Absorbed radiation causes heat; the amount depends on the intensity and duration of exposure.
- High energy photons can cause ionisation.
- Ultraviolet radiation, X-rays and gamma rays are all ionising radiations.
- Cells can be damaged by heat from absorbed radiation.
- Ionising radiation can damage cells when it is absorbed and can cause cancer.
- High intensity ionising radiation can destroy cells.

> **HT** • When ionising radiation strikes molecules it can make them more reactive.

The Earth

- The Earth is surrounded by a thin layer of atmosphere which allows light from the Sun to pass through.
- Radiation from the Sun allows plants to photosynthesize to produce glucose.
- Greenhouse gases trap electromagnetic radiation trying to leave the Earth.
- An increase in the amount of carbon dioxide in the atmosphere traps more heat.
- The temperature on the Earth's surface is often high enough for water to be liquid.
- The atmosphere contains oxygen (from photosynthesis), which is needed by animals for respiration.
- The ozone is a thin layer of gas in the atmosphere.

> **HT** • The ozone layer absorbs ultraviolet radiation from the Sun and protects living organisms from its harmful effects.

- Global warming could result in extreme weather conditions, rising sea levels and the extinction of some species (including crops and food sources).

The Carbon Cycle

- The materials that living things are made from are used over and over again.
- Carbon is a vital element in all the molecules that living things are made from.
- The continual recycling of compounds containing carbon is called the carbon cycle.
- The amount of carbon dioxide in the atmosphere had remained fairly constant for thousands of years.
- Decomposers break down dead material and release carbon dioxide back into the atmosphere.
- Burning fossil fuels and forests for energy releases carbon dioxide into the atmosphere.

Ideas about Science

Correlation and Cause

- A correlation (matching pattern) between a factor and an outcome suggests that one may cause or influence the other.

> **HT** • A correlation between a factor does not always mean that one causes the other.

Risk

- Any activity contains a certain risk of accident or harm.

> **HT** • The size of risk can sometimes be assessed by measuring its chance of occurring over a given time period.
> • The perceived risk is often very different from the actual risk.
> • The ALARA principle suggests a balance between risk and benefit.

Life on Earth

We are continually searching for an answer to the question of how life on Earth began and how different species evolved. This module looks at…

- how life on Earth began
- how creatures have evolved over time
- evolution by natural selection
- selective breeding
- nervous and communication systems.

Life on Earth

Life on Earth began about 3500 million years ago, and during that time there has been a large number of species living on the Earth. A species is a group of organisms which can freely breed with each other to produce fertile offspring.

We know that the very first living things developed from simple molecules that could copy or replicate themselves. However, it is not known whether the molecules were produced by conditions on Earth at the time (due to harsh surface conditions, or in deep sea vents) or whether the molecules arrived on Earth from an external source, e.g. a comet hitting the Earth.

There have been experiments that simulated the harsh conditions on Earth millions of years ago, which have led to simple organic molecules developing. There is also evidence of simple organic molecules existing in gas clouds in space and in comets.

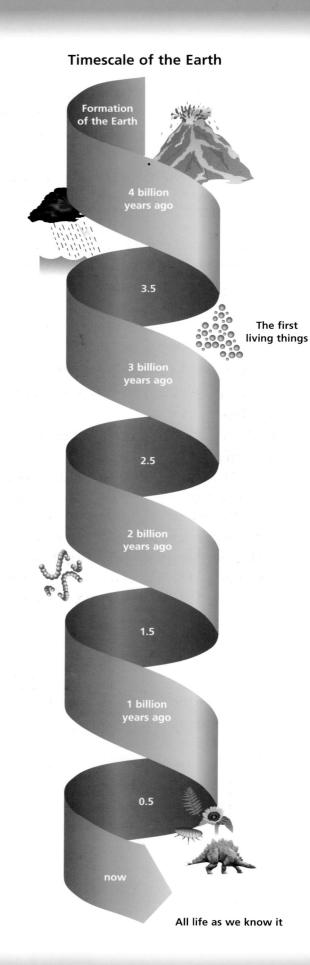

Timescale of the Earth

Formation of the Earth

4 billion years ago

3.5

The first living things

3 billion years ago

2.5

2 billion years ago

1.5

1 billion years ago

0.5

now

All life as we know it

The Beginning of Life

Whilst scientists are still investigating how life began on Earth, there is evidence to suggest that all existing organisms share certain traits, including cellular structure and genetic code.

This would mean that all existing organisms share a **common ancestor**, and have evolved from very simple living things, which had already developed the most fundamental cellular process. There are two sources of evidence to support this hypothesis.

1 The Fossil Record

Fossils are the remains of plants or animals from many years ago which are found in rock.

Fossils indicate the history of species and can show the evolutionary changes in organisms over millions of years. They can be formed...

- from the hard parts of animals that do not decay easily
- from parts of animals and plants which have not decayed because one or more of the conditions needed for decay were absent e.g. oxygen, moisture, temperature or correct pH levels
- from the soft parts of organisms which can be replaced by minerals as they decay. This can preserve the traces of footprints, burrows or rootlets.

Evolution of Ammonites

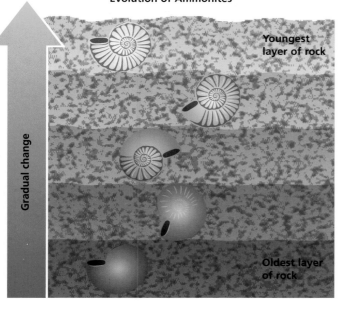

Gradual change

Youngest layer of rock

Oldest layer of rock

2 DNA Evidence

Not every dead organism has been preserved as a fossil. However, analysing the DNA of both living organisms and fossilised specimens shows similarities and differences, and this can be used to fill in gaps that exist in the fossil record. The more shared genes organisms have, the more closely related they are.

Comparing the gene sequences of organisms reveals that some organisms have a high degree of similarity in their DNA even with organisms that they are less obviously related to.

For example, human DNA sequences share 98.8% of a chimpanzee's DNA. The chimpanzee is our nearest genetic relative. A mouse, on the other hand, which appears very dissimilar from humans, shares 85% of a chimpanzee's DNA.

Mouse   Chimpanzee   Human

In whatever way life initially started, it is only through **evolution by natural selection** that life on the planet is as it is today. If the conditions on Earth had been different, at any time, to what they actually were, then evolution by natural selection could have produced very different results.

Life on Earth

Evolution by Natural Selection

Evolution is the slow, continual change in a population over a large number of generations. It may result in the formation of a new species, the members of which are better adapted to their environment.

Evolution occurs due to **natural selection**. This is where individuals in a population have certain characteristics which improve their chances of survival in their physical environment. They are therefore more likely to live to adulthood and reproduce, passing on their favourable characteristics to their offspring. Individuals with poorly fitting characteristics are less likely to survive and reproduce.

So the number of individuals with the favourable traits increases whilst the number of those with unfavourable traits decreases.

There are four key points to remember in terms of natural selection:

1. Individuals within a population show **variation**, i.e. differences due to their genes.

2. There is **competition** between individuals for food and mates, etc. Also predation and disease keeps population sizes constant in spite of the production of many offspring.

3. Individuals which are **better adapted** to the environment are more likely to survive, breed successfully and produce offspring. This is termed **survival of the fittest**.

4. These survivors will **pass on their genes** to their offspring resulting in the evolution of an improved organism over generations.

Natural selection relies on variation. Variation in individuals is caused by the **environment** and **genes**.

However, *only* a genetic variation can be passed on. For example, if you had an accident and lost one of your fingers this new characteristic would not be passed on to your offspring; this is an example of **environmental variation**.

Peppered Moths are naturally pale and speckled in colour. This means they are well camouflaged against the bark of silver birch trees.

However, during the Industrial Revolution, air pollution from the factories and mills discoloured the bark of the trees with soot and natural selection led to a new variety of Peppered moth.

1. **Variation** – Some Peppered Moths, about 10%, were naturally darker than others due to their genes.
2. **Competition** – The darker-coloured moths and paler moths had to compete for food and water.
3. **Better adapted** – The darker moths were better camouflaged against the blackened bark of trees and soot on buildings. The paler moths were much more easily seen by birds and were therefore eaten.
4. **Passing on genes** – The darker moths were more likely to survive and breed, passing on their blacker genes.

In the mid-1950s the Government passed the Clean Air Act. This dramatically reduced air pollution and so more silver birch trees stayed 'silver'. This meant that the pale variety (now about 10% of population) had an advantage and so, due to natural selection, began to grow again in numbers. Today, the presence of the pale variety of Peppered Moth is regarded as a marker for clean air.

Peppered Moth

Black Peppered Moth

Gene Mutation

When a change occurs in a gene it is called a **mutation**.

Mutations take place in DNA. Most of the time the mutations are corrected. However, occasionally a mutation can take place that alters the properties of a protein and can influence the development of an organism (see p.6).

If this happens in a sex cell then the mutated gene can be passed on to the offspring, which may show new characteristics.

Section of Gene

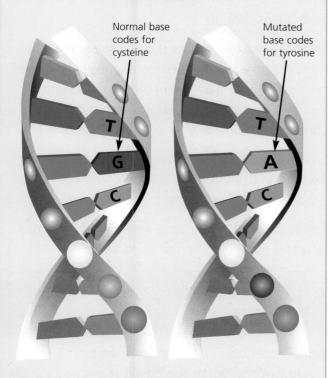

Normal base codes for cysteine

Mutated base codes for tyrosine

A new species can be produced through the combined effects of mutations, environmental changes and natural selection.

Selective Breeding

Selective breeding is where animals with certain traits are deliberately mated to produce offspring with certain desirable characteristics. Selective breeding can produce two outcomes (see opposite):

1 **Creating New Varieties of Organism**

e.g. Dalmatian dogs.

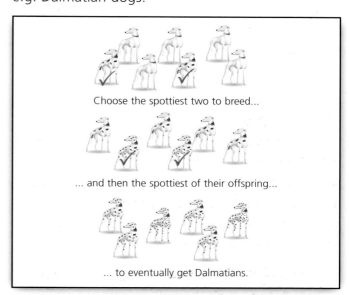

Choose the spottiest two to breed...

... and then the spottiest of their offspring...

... to eventually get Dalmatians.

2 **Increasing the Yields of Animals and Plants**

Some breeds of cattle have been bred to produce high yields of milk or milk with a high fat content.

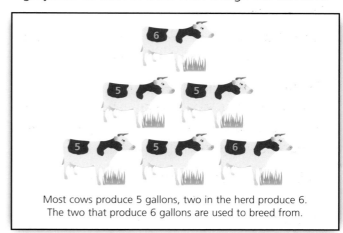

Most cows produce 5 gallons, two in the herd produce 6. The two that produce 6 gallons are used to breed from.

Improved crops can be obtained by selective breeding programmes, although this happens over a very long period of time.

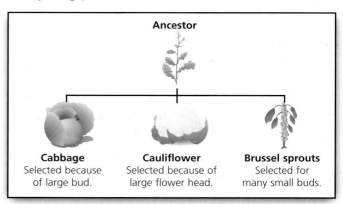

Ancestor

Cabbage	**Cauliflower**	**Brussel sprouts**
Selected because of large bud.	Selected because of large flower head.	Selected for many small buds.

Life on Earth

The Evolution of Humans

The similarities between great apes and humans have been obvious to mankind for some time, and it is thought that they shared a **common ancestor**. Although the fossil records for human ancestors is sparse, it was through the investigation of the fossilised remains that scientists built up a human family tree showing human evolution.

A **Hominid** is any member of the biological family Hominidea (the 'great apes') including humans, gorillas and orang-utans. During evolution, the hominid family diverged (branched) and several Homo species (Homo being Latin for 'person') developed.

In modern classification, *Homo sapiens* is the *only* living species of its type. There were other Homo species, all of which are now extinct. While some of these other species might have been ancestors of Homo sapiens, it is likely that others were '**cousins**', who evolved away from our ancestral line.

Members of the Homo group include…
- *Homo habilis* – evidence exists that they were the earliest ancestor. They made and used simple tools from stone and animal bone.
- *Homo erectus* – had large brains and may have used fire to cook their food.
- *Homo sapiens* – humans today.
- *Homo neanderthalensis* – a close cousin of *Homo sapiens*.

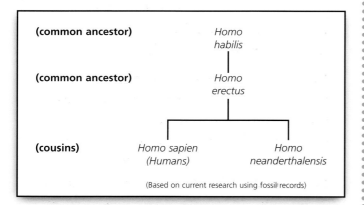

(common ancestor)	*Homo habilis*	
(common ancestor)	*Homo erectus*	
(cousins)	*Homo sapien (Humans)*	*Homo neanderthalensis*

(Based on current research using fossil records)

Over a period of 300 million years, the brain size of hominids increased. This is likely to be due to natural selection, as there is a rough correlation

between brain size and intelligence. Individuals with larger brains would have had a greater intellectual capacity (ability to process information from the environment). This would give them an advantage over those with smaller brains, making them more likely to survive and pass on their genes onto their offspring.

Based on this correlation, it was initially thought that brain size would have increased first and then hominids would have learned to walk upright. However, fossil evidence suggests that walking upright came first.

This shows how important new observations and data are in helping to establish the reliability of an explanation and improve our scientific understanding:

If new observations or data agree with a theory it increases confidence in the explanation.

> **HT** However, it does not necessarily prove that the theory is correct.

If new observations or data disagree with a theory, it indicates that either the observations or data are wrong, or the theory is wrong.

> **HT** This, therefore, may decrease our confidence in the explanation.

In the latter situation, further investigations are carried out to establish where the error lies. If the new observations or data prove to be reliable, then the existing theory will be revised or changed. This is how scientific explanations change and develop over time.

Life on Earth

Origins of Life

How life on Earth began is a question that has been debated by different religions and scientists for years.

In general terms, religions believe that God, or a creator, created all life. Scientists, on the other hand, noted how organisms looked similar to each other, and over the years have developed testable theories to try to explain these similarities.

Theory of Inheritance of Acquired Characteristics

Jean-Baptiste Lamarck believed that an animal evolved within its lifetime. He put forward the hypothesis that the more an animal used a part of its body, the more likely it would be that it would adapt to be better at that job. For example, a giraffe stretching for leaves on a tall tree would develop a long neck, a characteristic which would then be passed onto its offspring.

Then later, Weismann, a scientist, experimented on mice. He cut their tails off and then bred them. However, he found that the tail-less mice produced offspring with tails. This new data conflicted with Lamarck's explanation and cast doubt on his theory. Lamarck countered this by saying that experiments like Weismann's did not count because it was a deliberate mutation; only those situations where the animal itself desired a change were valid. However, this new evidence led to Lamarck's theory being rejected.

Lamarck is an example of a scientist using imagination and creativity to develop an explanation.

HT A scientific explanation is not abandoned as soon as new data is found that conflicts with it for lots of reasons: the new data may be incorrect; explanations based on new data have the potential to run into problems quickly; lots of scientists will have based work on the existing explanation and will be inclined to stick with what has served them well in the past. Therefore, a new explanation is only likely to replace it when it has been tried and tested, and proven to be reliable.

Evolution by Natural Selection

In the 1830s, Charles Darwin consolidated existing ideas about evolution and created a testable theory of how evolution takes place. His work was based on observable evidence, e.g. studies of the different types of finch on the Galapagos Islands.

By collecting data, Darwin made four important observations which were at the heart of his theory of evolution: variety, competition, survival of the fittest, and passing on desirable characteristics to the next generation (see p.60)

HT Darwin **linked these observations** and deduced that all organisms were involved in a struggle for survival in which only the best-adapted organisms would be able to survive, reproduce and pass on their characteristics. This formed the basis for his famous theory of 'Evolution by Natural Selection'.

There are many different theories and scientists cannot be absolutely certain about how life on Earth began; it is difficult to find evidence to prove any theory, and theories are based on the best evidence at the time. No one experienced the beginning of life on Earth so it is impossible to ever be certain how it began. Even today we are making new discoveries and developing our scientific knowledge.

Life on Earth

The Extinction of Species

Throughout the history of Earth, species of animals and plants have become **extinct** (they no longer exist anywhere on the planet), e.g. the Dodo.

The usual cause of extinction is a species' inability to adapt to change in the form of…
- increased competition
- new predators
- change in the environment
- new diseases.

There have been at least five **mass extinctions** in the history of life on Earth in which many species have disappeared in a relatively short period of geological time.

These extinctions have taken place in the last 0.5 billion years. Mass extinction occurs when a change to the environment happens so quickly, that animals and plants are not able to produce individuals able to cope with the change. For example, it is thought that the dinosaurs were killed when an asteroid hit the Earth, which would have caused dramatic, immediate environmental changes.

Human activity, whether directly or indirectly, has been responsible for the extinction of some species. Such human activity includes:
- The introduction of new predators or competition to areas where the animal or plant previously had no natural competitors or predators, e.g. the Mitten crab travelled in ballast tanks of ships from Asia to the UK. The crab eats native species of crab.
- Industrial activities increase the amount of greenhouse gases in the atmosphere, which are responsible for global warming.
- Deforestation clears whole habitats, increases the amount of carbon dioxide in the atmosphere and alters the carbon cycle.

If unchecked, these changes can and will cause species to become extinct.

Example:

Extinctions Caused Directly by Man:

The **Great Auk**. This sea bird lived in places like Canada, Iceland and Britain. They were hunted for food and their down was used for mattresses. The last pair of Great Auks was killed by hunters on July 3rd 1844. The auk only laid one egg a year and could not fly to escape, so was vulnerable to hunters.

Smallpox. This virus was declared eradicated (extinct) in 1980 by the World Health Organisation. The only examples of the virus are currently stored in two laboratories, one in America, the other in Russia. The virus was eradicated deliberately by man by mass vaccination (intentionally removing the habitat of the virus).

Extinctions Caused Indirectly by Man:

The **Philippine bare-backed fruit bat**. These bats lived on Negros Island in the Philippines. They were once so numerous that they left piles of droppings on the island. However, by the mid-1980s their habitat, lowland forest, was replaced by sugar cane plantations, and the bat became extinct.

The **Gould's Mouse**. This Australian animal, slightly smaller than a rat, disappeared rapidly after settlement by Europeans in the 1840s. They were thought to have been brought to extinction due to being hunted by cats, and killed by diseases from rats and mice (all introduced by man). They were also affected by changes to their habitat.

Maintaining Biodiversity

Every time a species becomes extinct, information stored in the organisms' genetic code is lost. There are now projects to prevent this, like the Kew Gardens Millennium Seed Bank Project, which aims to safeguard 24 000 plant species from around the globe against extinction. This is achieved by collecting and storing seeds from all over the world.

Extinctions mean less variety on Earth. Without this variety people would start to run out of food crops and medicines. Many medicines are developed from plants and animals, for example the foxglove was found to contain a chemical, digitalis, that could be used to treat heart disease.

There are potentially an unknown number of medicines existing in the genetic code of animals and plants living in areas such as the Amazon rainforest – an area which is losing 25 000 square kilometres a year to deforestation. By understanding how our actions can impact on biodiversity, scientists hope to discover ways to use the Earth's resources in a **sustainable** way, so that future generations can enjoy a similar diversity of living things.

Food Chains

Organisms do not live in isolation from one another. There is competition for resources between different species of animals or plants in the same habitat. Food chains can be used to show the direction of energy and material transfer between organisms, and which organisms are eating other organisms.

Example
Energy from the Sun enters the food chain when green plants absorb sunlight in order to photosynthesize. When animals eat the plants the energy passes from one organism to another up the food chain.

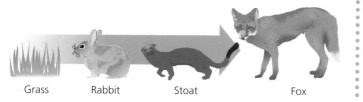

| Grass | Rabbit | Stoat | Fox |

The animals are all dependent upon each other and their environment. For example, if all the rabbits became extinct, then the stoat would be at risk of starving, which, in turn, would put the fox at risk. In reality, most animals are not just dependent upon one food source, so the stoats and foxes would not all die, but their numbers would probably be reduced, as competition for the remaining food sources would increase.

Food Webs

Food webs are drawn to show how all the food chains in a given habitat are inter-related. In practice these can be very complicated because many animals have varied diets.

Food Web

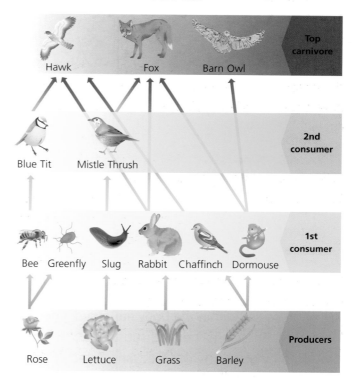

Changes to the environment can alter numbers in the food web. For example, a small change in the amount of rain could reduce the amount of lettuces and cause reductions in numbers of slugs. If the changes are too great for the natural variation within a population to accommodate, then organisms will die out before they can reproduce. The population will decline and eventually become extinct.

Life on Earth

Nervous and Communication Systems

The evolution of multi-cellular organisms eventually led to specialised cells working together as tissue. Different tissues working together formed organs, and collections of organs working together formed organ systems.

This led to the development of **nervous** and **hormonal** communication systems. There are several differences between the messages in the two systems:

Nerve Impulses
- Electrical impulses in nerves
- Rapid action
- Last a short time.

Hormone Signals
- Chemical messages in blood
- Slow action
- Last a long time.

> **HT** The maintenance of a constant internal body environment (temperature, water balance etc) is called **homeostasis**.
>
> The human body uses both nervous signals and hormonal signals to ensure the body systems are stable.

Hormone Communication

Many processes within the body are coordinated by hormones. These are chemical substances, produced by glands, which are transported around the body by the bloodstream. Hormones regulate the functions of many organs and cells.

Control of **hormones** is far slower and comparatively longer-lasting than nervous impulses, because the hormones travel to the relevant effector in the bloodstream. It takes approximately 10 seconds for blood to travel once around the body.

Example 1: Human Fertility

A woman naturally produces hormones that cause the maturation and release of an egg from her ovaries, and also cause changes in the thickness of the lining of her womb. The hormones are produced by the pituitary gland and the ovaries.

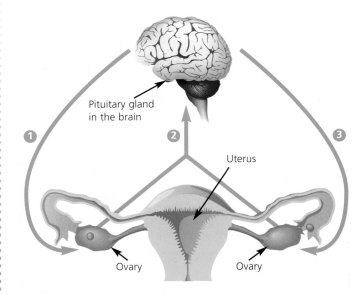

Pituitary gland in the brain

Uterus

Ovary   Ovary

1. Follicle stimulating hormone (FSH) from the pituitary gland causes the ovaries to produce oestrogen and an egg to mature.
2. Oestrogen, produced in the ovaries, inhibits the production of FSH and causes the production of luteinising hormone (LH).
3. LH, also from the pituitary gland, stimulates the release of an egg in the middle of the menstrual cycle.

Example 2: Insulin

Insulin is a hormone produced by the pancreas; its level in the blood is governed by the amount of glucose in the blood.

If the concentration of glucose increases, insulin is then released into the bloodstream.

The presence of insulin causes cells (which need glucose for respiration) to take in the glucose. Any additional glucose is then stored as glycogen.

The transportation (movement) of glucose is governed by the circulatory system.

The Central Nervous System

The nervous system is based around sensor (receptor) cells that detect **stimuli**, and effector cells which **respond** to the stimuli. Nerve cells (neurones) connect the sensor cells (e.g. in eyes, ears and skin) and effector cells (e.g. muscles / glands) together.

Neurones are specially adapted cells that can carry an electrical signal, e.g. a nerve impulse.

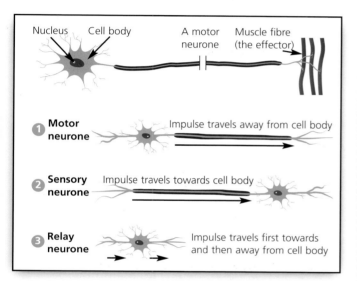

The coordination of the nervous system in humans, and other vertebrates, is carried out by the spinal cord and the brain. This is referred to as the **central nervous system**. Messages are sent via electrical impulses which allow fast, short-lived responses.

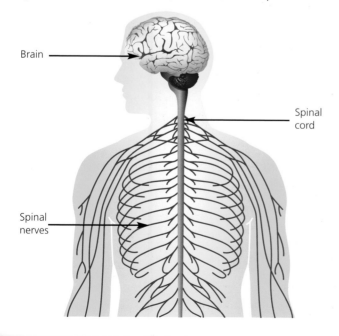

Example 1: Removing your Hand from a Pin – Involuntary Reflex Action

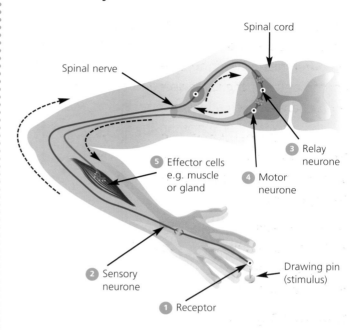

1. A receptor is stimulated by the drawing pin (stimulus)...
2. ... causing impulses to pass along a sensory neurone into the spinal cord.
3. The sensory neurone synapses (communicates) with a relay neurone, by-passing the brain.
4. The relay neurone synapses with a motor neurone, sending impulses down it...
5. ... to the muscles (effectors) causing them to contract and remove the hand in response to the sharp drawing pin.

Example 2: Turning Down Loud Music – Voluntary Reaction

Sound-sensitive receptors in the ear detect loud music.

The sensory neurones then pass an electrical signal to the central nervous system where the information is processed.

A response, in the form of another electrical signal, is sent by the motor neurone to the effector cells in the muscles in the arms and fingers.

The arm and finger muscles respond by covering the ears to try and block the sound and then turning the volume down.

Life on Earth – Summary

Science Explanations

The Interdependence of Living Things

- A food web can show which organisms eat other organisms in a particular habitat.
- Different species in a particular habitat often compete for the same space or food source.
- A change which affects one species in a food web also affects other species in the same food web.
- Ecosystems can often adjust to changes but large disruptions may change an ecosystem permanently.

Maintenance of Life

- Organisms need water, food and light to survive.
- Organisms need to avoid harmful chemicals, predators and extreme temperatures in order to survive.
- They are more likely to survive if they can sense what they need, or need to avoid, in their surroundings.
- Multi-cellular organisms have sensor cells and effector cells.
- Multi-cellular animals have nervous systems.
- Nervous systems comprise nerve cells (neurones) which link sensor cells to effector cells.
- In humans they are linked via the central nervous system (spinal cord and brain).
- Hormones are chemicals which travel in the blood and bring about slower, longer-lasting responses.

Theory of Evolution by Natural Selection

> **HT**
> - Nervous and hormonal communication systems are involved in maintaining a constant internal environment (homeostasis).

- The first living things developed about 3 500 million years ago from molecules that could copy themselves.
- The molecules were produced in the conditions on Earth at the time.
- Evolution occurs due to natural selection.

- If conditions on Earth had been different from what they were, natural selection could have produced very different results.
- There is variation between individuals of the same species.
- Individuals with certain characteristics have a better chance of surviving, and reproducing, if the environment changes or vital resources become scarce.
- There will be more individuals with these characteristics in the next generation, and so on.
- Selective breeding involves making deliberate selections based on desirable characteristics.
- New species have evolved over a very long period of time.

> **HT**
> - Genes can be changed by mutation.
> - Mutation can cause cancer cells.
> - Mutated genes in sex cells can be passed onto offspring and produce new characteristics.

- A large change in the environment may cause an entire species to become extinct.

> **HT**
> - A new species can be produced by the combined effects of mutations, environmental changes and natural selection.

Ideas about Science

Scientific Explanations

- For some scientific questions, there is not a definite answer yet.
- An observation that agrees with a theory increases confidence in it.
- An observation that disagrees with a theory indicates that either the observation or the theory is wrong.
- Explanations cannot simply be deduced from the available data – personal background, experience or interests may influence judgements.

Module C3

Different farming methods and the chemicals and additives that are added to our food can affect our health. This module looks at...

- issues facing farmers in the production of large amounts of good quality food
- chemicals found in foods: both natural chemicals and additives
- the role of the Food Standards Agency
- what happens to our food when we eat it
- health risks associated with eating.

The Nitrogen Cycle

Nitrogen is a vital element in all living things. It is used in the production of amino acids and proteins, which are needed for plants and animals to grow. Fertile soil containing a range of nutrients is needed for crops to grow. There is a continual cycle of elements through consumption of living organisms and decay. This is clearly seen in the nitrogen cycle, which shows how nitrogen and its compounds are recycled in nature.

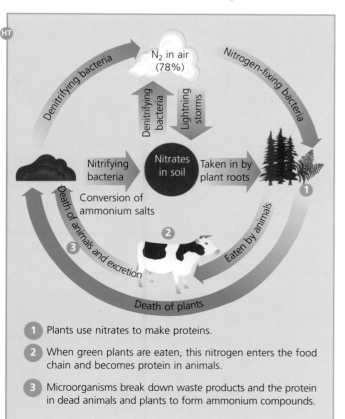

1. Plants use nitrates to make proteins.

2. When green plants are eaten, this nitrogen enters the food chain and becomes protein in animals.

3. Microorganisms break down waste products and the protein in dead animals and plants to form ammonium compounds.

Intensive and Organic Farming

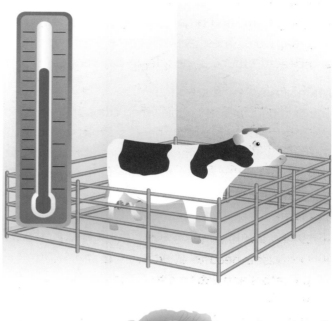

Farmers are increasingly faced with the challenge of producing greater quantities of food at lower costs. To help achieve this, farmers can use **intensive farming** practices which include the use of fertilisers, pesticides and herbicides. They can also keep animals in carefully controlled environments where their temperature and movement are limited. However, some people find this morally unacceptable as the animals have a poor quality of life.

Organic farming uses more natural methods which have little environmental impact. However, the costs are higher as more farm workers need to be employed.

Farms must pass the UK National, and International Standards if they want to be recognised as organic farms; the Soil Association is one of the agencies that monitors the standards of these farms.

Food Matters

Farming Issues

There are several issues facing farming today which intensive farms and organic farms try to solve in different ways. These can affect the environment, and benefit groups of people, in different ways.

Maintaining Fertile Soil

The land becomes less fertile when crops are harvested because plants remove nutrients such as nitrogen from the soil and they are not returned through the natural process of decay. Intensive farmers use manufactured fertilisers to replace the lost nitrogen compounds and other nutrients. Organic farmers use manure from animals to add nutrients to the soil. They also rotate their crops, e.g. grass / clover → wheat → root crops (beet) → grass / clover.

> **HT** Harvested crops also remove **potassium** and **phosphorus** from the soil.

Crop Yields

Pests (such as insects) may carry disease and can damage crops. This means that fewer crops are produced or there is a lower yield. Intensive farms use **pesticides** (chemicals that kill the pests) while organic farmers use **biological control** (introduction of a predator). Intensive farms generally produce high yields at low cost, which benefits consumers. Organic farms are more labour intensive and produce lower yields at higher costs.

The Environment (Intensive)

Intensive farms are often small, leaving more room for woodland. However, hedgerows are often removed to create larger fields, to maximise the amount of crops planted per area of land. The farmers' use of fertilisers can lead to **eutrophication** and pesticides can harm other organisms that are not pests. Pesticides can accumulate in the food chain passing the toxins to animals further up the chain. Over 50% of the energy used in intensive farming is used to make fertilisers. Most of this energy comes from burning fossil fuels (see p.18).

The Environment (Organic)

Organic farms have smaller fields with less destruction of hedgerows. Food chains are not affected. They do not use pesticides and fertilisers so there is less eutrophication, and there is more local employment. This is more **sustainable development**.

> **HT** There is a difference between what can be done and what should be done and different social and economic circumstances also need to be considered (see p.11).

Chemicals in Living Things

Many chemicals in living organisms are natural polymers, (see p.44), e.g. carbohydrates and proteins. Cellulose, starch and sugars are carbohydrates which contain the elements carbon, hydrogen and oxygen, e.g. glucose $C_6H_{12}O_6$.

Glucose molecules join together in a long chain to form starch.

Individual sugar molecules (glucose) → Huge, long chains of identical sugar molecules (starch).

Cellulose is formed when the glucose molecules form long chains which are cross-linked.

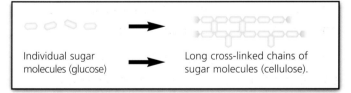

Individual sugar molecules (glucose) → Long cross-linked chains of sugar molecules (cellulose).

Proteins are polymers made from long chains of amino acids. They contain the elements carbon, hydrogen, oxygen, nitrogen and sometimes other elements such as sulfur.

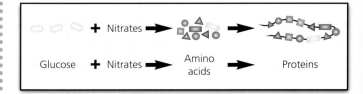

Glucose + Nitrates → Amino acids → Proteins

Chemicals in Food

Chemicals, or additives, are added to food for a number of reasons (see table below):

Additive	Reason
Colouring	Replaces colour lost during processing or storage. Colourful food looks more attractive.
Flavouring	Gives a particular taste or flavour. Replaces flavours lost during processing.
Emulsifier	Used to mix together ingredients that would normally separate, e.g. oil and water.
Stabiliser	Helps to stop ingredients from separating again.
Preservative	Stops mould or bacteria growing in food, so foods are kept safe and fresher for longer.
Sweetener	Used to reduce the amount of sugar added to processed foods and drinks.
Antioxidant	Added to foods containing fats or oils to stop them from reacting with oxygen in the air.

Health Concerns

If an additive has an **E number**, this means it has passed a safety test and it is safe to use in the UK and the rest of the European Union.

However, there are some health concerns about the use of food additives. Although not all scientists agree, some think, for example, that the flavouring monosodium glutamate (E621), can have harmful effects, and that sodium benzoate (E211) and carmoisine (E122) can be linked to hyperactivity and skin problems.

Increased consumption of E numbers, especially amongst children, is also thought to affect sleep patterns, behaviour, ability to concentrate, and even IQ levels.

Sweeties

INGREDIENTS:
Sugar, Milk, Cocoa Butter, Modified starch, Colours (E104 Quinoline Yellow, E110 Sunset Yellow FCF, E120 Carminic acid, E122 Carmoisine, E124 Cochineal Red A, E133 Brilliant Blue FCF, E171 Titanium dioxide), Glazing agents (E901 Beeswax, E903 Carnauba wax), Flavouring.

Food Matters

The Food We Eat

Many plants are eaten for food. Some can be eaten raw, e.g. fruit and vegetables, but there are some plants which contain natural chemicals which may be toxic, and cause harm if they are not cooked properly.

Some of these chemicals may also give rise to allergies in some people. Examples are listed in the table below:

Plant	Natural Chemical	Effect
Cassava (a woody shrub)	Poisonous compounds release cyanide	Cyanide poisoning if eaten raw. Heating removes the toxin.
Wheat	Gluten	Damages the small intestine in people who suffer from intolerance (known as coeliac disease).
Peanuts	Proteins in the nuts	Allergic reaction from fresh, cooked and roasted peanuts as the proteins are not destroyed by cooking.

There are many opportunities for harmful chemicals to get into our food, and it is impossible for any food to be completely safe:

- Contamination during storage – moulds growing on cereals, dried fruit and nuts can produce a carcinogen called aflatoxin.
- The use of pesticides and herbicides by farmers can mean that chemicals sprayed onto crops may remain in the products we eat.
- Food processing and cooking may produce harmful chemicals.
- Poor storage of cooked food may result in contamination by bacteria, which can lead to **food poisoning**.

Organic farming and the way in which food is stored and processed can reduce the risks of harmful chemicals getting into the food.

There are also a number of steps that people can take to reduce their exposure to harmful chemicals. These include…

- keeping a hygienic kitchen and quickly disposing of waste food
- cooking food properly
- not re-freezing previously frozen meats
- regularly cleaning out the fridge to avoid keeping cooked foods too long
- reading food labels – particularly important for people who suffer from coeliac disease or have known allergies.

The **risk** from different chemicals in our food can vary from person to person. For example, most of the time eating out is a low-risk activity because there are laws about food hygiene, and kitchens must meet Health and Safety standards. However, it is not always possible to know all the ingredients that have gone into preparing food. Therefore, if you are allergic to a common ingredient in food such as wheat, eggs, nuts, etc. eating out may be a higher risk for you than for other people.

Food Standards Agency

The Food Standards Agency (FSA) is an independent food safety watchdog set up by an Act of Parliament in 2000.

The FSA helps to make sure that our food is safe, healthy and fairly marketed. It also makes sure that food producers are acting within the law. The FSA promotes healthy eating and aims to minimise illnesses such as food poisoning. It makes sure that food labels are clear and that they say exactly what is in the food.

The food labels help people to decide whether or not to buy the product. For example, coeliacs look for labels that say 'gluten free'; and vegetarians look to see if the food contains any animal products. (Some foods also state 'suitable for vegetarians'.)

The FSA wants to give the public the most up-to-date information about food safety. In order to do this the agency employs scientists to carry out research into food issues such as **genetically modified** (GM) foods.

Sometimes the research findings are controversial and the results are uncertain. Scientists may even disagree about what the results actually mean. Further problems may be encountered from manufacturers who may not want to accept the research findings, as it may not be in their economic interest.

If there is any doubt about food safety then one of the scientific advisory committees is asked to carry out a risk assessment. They must decide...

- if the food contains any chemicals that could cause harm
- how harmful the chemicals are
- how much of the food must be eaten before it is likely to harm people
- if any groups of people are particularly vulnerable, e.g. the elderly, children, or those suffering from a previous illnesses.

HT The outcome of a risk assessment is often based on experience gained from people or animals eating the food.

Sometimes the scientific evidence is uncertain and the risk is unknown, in which case the **precautionary principle** is applied. Both experts and the public are consulted before the regulators make a decision about food safety.

They have to weigh up the costs and benefits of any decision, as the priority is to protect public safety and not just let the new foods be mass produced and put on the market.

For example, many people ask the question, 'Are GM foods safe to eat?'

For many GM foods, scientists simply do not know enough about the science of altering genes, which may lead to health problems in the future. There is also not much data yet on the potential risks to humans, and this is why the precautionary principle is sometimes applied.

Food Matters

Digestion

When we eat food, it gets digested.

Physical digestion includes chewing and squeezing food in the stomach. This breaks the food into smaller pieces so that it can pass more easily through the gut, and increases the surface area of the food to help enzymes work more quickly.

Chemical digestion uses enzymes to break down the large insoluble molecules into smaller soluble molecules.

The smaller molecules can diffuse through the walls of the small intestines into the blood, where they are transported to different parts of the body.

Enzymes in the saliva and stomach break down starch into glucose.

Huge, long chains of identical sugar molecules (starch).

Individual sugar molecules (glucose)

Enzymes in the small intestine break down proteins into amino acids.

Huge, long chains of different amino acids.

Amino acids

The glucose is used in respiration to release energy and the amino acids are used to build new cells and repair damaged ones.

Amino acids are taken from the bloodstream by cells as they grow. The amino acids build up in the cells until proteins are made. Many parts of the body, including muscle, tendons, skin, hair, and haemoglobin in the blood, consist mainly of proteins.

In a healthy person the excess amino acids are transported to the liver where they are broken down to form urea. Urea is transported in the blood to the kidneys where it is filtered out before being excreted in urine. If the liver did not function correctly, harmful chemicals could be formed during the breakdown of the amino acids.

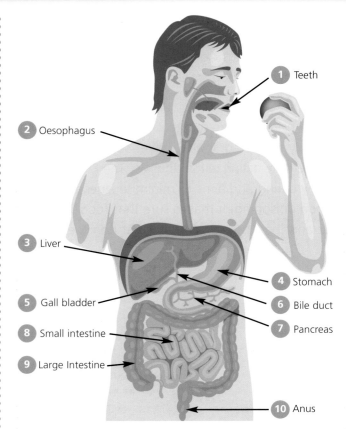

1. Teeth
2. Oesophagus
3. Liver
4. Stomach
5. Gall bladder
6. Bile duct
7. Pancreas
8. Small intestine
9. Large Intestine
10. Anus

1. **Teeth** – used for grinding up food.
2. **Oesophagus** – carries food from the mouth to the stomach.
3. **Liver** – produces bile which helps digest fat.
4. **Stomach** – stores food. It produces an enzyme to help digest food. Hydrochloric acid is released by cells in the wall of the stomach. It kills bacteria and provides the best conditions for the enzyme to work.
5. **Gall bladder** – stores bile, before releasing it into the small intestine.
6. **Bile duct** – takes bile from the gall bladder to the small intestine.
7. **Pancreas** – produces enzymes which are released into the small intestine to help digest food.
8. **Small intestine** – produces more enzymes which complete the chemical digestion of food. The small, soluble molecules produced by digestion are absorbed by the small intestine.
9. **Large intestine** – excess water from the contents of the intestines is reabsorbed into the blood here. Faeces are stored before passing out of the body.
10. **Anus** – faeces leave the body here.

Importance of a Healthy Diet

In order to remain healthy it is important to eat a balanced diet. This includes…

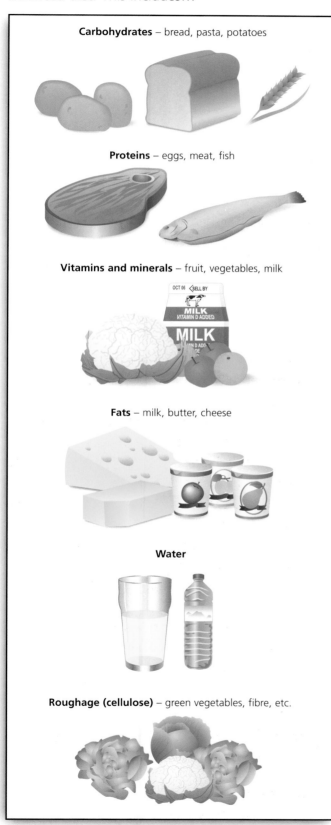

Carbohydrates – bread, pasta, potatoes

Proteins – eggs, meat, fish

Vitamins and minerals – fruit, vegetables, milk

OCT 06   SELL BY
MILK
VITAMIN D ADDED
MILK

Fats – milk, butter, cheese

Water

Roughage (cellulose) – green vegetables, fibre, etc.

Eating the wrong foods can lead to many different types of diseases.

For example, in the UK, **obesity** (being very overweight) is now a major problem, even amongst children. The main cause is eating too much, especially fatty, sugary foods, and not exercising enough.

Even though the link between heart disease and obesity is well known, many people still choose to over-eat and do not exercise. There are a number of reasons for this; people often think that it will not happen to them and that the short-term benefits outweigh the risks:

- foods that contain a lot of fat, salt and sugar such as crisps, soft drinks and sweets taste good
- fruit and vegetables can be expensive to buy
- exercising is hard work and people cannot be bothered
- processed microwave meals are quick and easy
- making meals from fresh ingredients takes time.

HT Obese people are endangering their health and increasing their chances of developing heart disease, cancer and diabetes.

If you eat a lot of the wrong type of foods, you may be putting yourself at risk of becoming obese. Questions you might ask yourself include…

- how healthy is my lifestyle?
- is there a family history of cancer, heart disease or diabetes, etc?
- am I in a high risk age group?

If you are at high risk and choose not to change your lifestyle, then you may later pay the consequences of poor health.

Food Matters

Diabetes

Diabetes is a disease that is caused by the pancreas not producing and releasing enough **insulin**, which allows the blood sugar level to fluctuate. This can lead to a person's blood sugar level rising fatally high, resulting in a coma, and even death.

Many processed foods contain high levels of sugar, which is quickly absorbed into the bloodstream, causing a rapid rise in the blood sugar level.

Even though there is some evidence to suggest that there is a link between diabetes and poor diet, many people still eat too much processed food.

There are two types of diabetes:

- **Type 1 diabetes** is where the pancreas stops producing insulin altogether as the special cells in the pancreas are destroyed. This is more likely to start in young people and the blood sugar level can be controlled by injecting insulin.
- **Type 2 diabetes** is where the pancreas does not make enough insulin or the cells do not respond. This can often be treated by diet and exercise although medicine and insulin injections are usually also needed.

The latter type of diabetes is late-onset diabetes and is more likely to start in older people. However, it is now also being seen in younger people. This is because there are more young people who are obese; this group of people has a higher **risk factor** than those who are the correct weight and have regular exercise. Other risk factors include genetics and age, for example, some ethnic minority groups develop type 2 diabetes at a younger age.

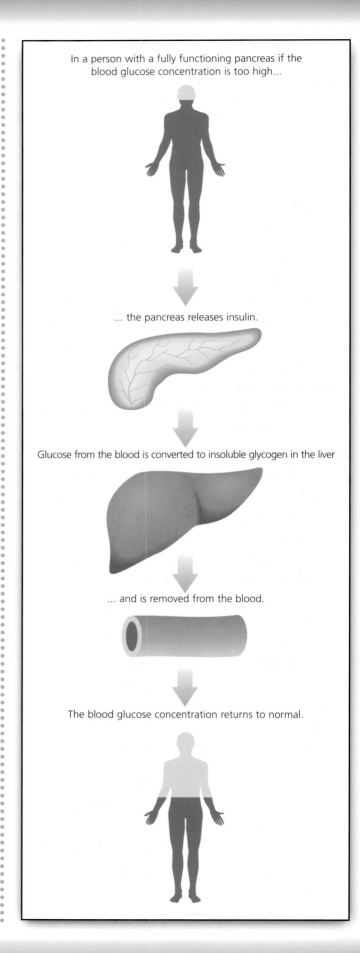

In a person with a fully functioning pancreas if the blood glucose concentration is too high...

... the pancreas releases insulin.

Glucose from the blood is converted to insoluble glycogen in the liver

... and is removed from the blood.

The blood glucose concentration returns to normal.

Food Matters – Summary

Science Explanations

Chemical Cycles

- Decomposers (microorganisms) break down the dead bodies of plants and animals. They play a very important role in the recycling of materials.
- Protein molecules are important in all living cells. They contain nitrogen atoms.

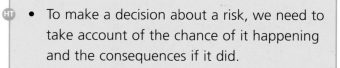

- Compounds containing nitrogen are continually cycled. This process is known as the nitrogen cycle.
- Potassium and phosphorus are important in living cells. They are also continually recycled.

- Farmers reuse the same land to grow plants and rear animals for food.
- The removal of nitrogen from the soil by farming makes it less fertile.

Maintenance of Life

- Animals, including humans, need a balanced diet including proteins, carbohydrates, fats, minerals, vitamins, and water.
- Large insoluble molecules are broken down in the gut by enzymes to form small soluble molecules.
- Starch is digested into glucose.
- Protein is digested into amino acids.
- The small molecules pass through the wall of the small intestine into the blood, which transports them to all the cells of the body.
- The cells produce toxic waste, which must be disposed of.
- Carbon dioxide is the by-product of respiration and is transported to the lungs where it is exhaled.
- Urea, produced by the breakdown of amino acids in the liver, is excreted from the body by the kidneys in urine.
- Undigested food never enters the bloodstream; it passes through the gut and leaves the body as faeces.

Ideas about Science

Risk

- Everything we do carries a risk of accident or harm; nothing is risk free.
- New technologies based on science often introduce new risks.
- Risk can often be assessed over a period of time.

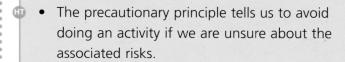

- To make a decision about a risk, we need to take account of the chance of it happening and the consequences if it did.

- People are willing to accept risk if they enjoy, or benefit from, the associated activity.
- People are more willing to accept risk associated with the things they choose to do rather than the things they must do.

- The precautionary principle tells us to avoid doing an activity if we are unsure about the associated risks.

Science and Technology

- The benefits of science-based technology need to be weighed against the costs.
- Scientists may identify unintended impacts of human activity on the environment. Sustainable development is concerned with using natural resources to reduce the impact.
- Scientific research is subject to official regulations and laws. There are laws about how farmers produce food, how the food is processed, how it is sold and what goes on the food label.
- Social and economic contexts play a part in accepting or rejecting applications in science.

Radioactive Materials

Radiation has many beneficial uses as well as dangers. This module looks at...

- ionising radiation
- radioactive decay and half-lives
- the dangers and uses of radiation
- how electricity is generated
- nuclear fission.

Atoms and Elements

All elements are made of atoms; each element contains only one type of atom. All atoms contain a nucleus and electrons. The nucleus is made from protons and neutrons with the one exception of hydrogen (the lightest element), which has no neutrons; just one proton and one electron.

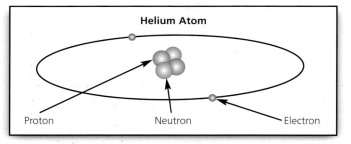

Helium Atom

Proton   Neutron   Electron

Some elements give out **ionising radiation** all the time, we call these elements **radioactive**. Neither chemical reactions nor physical processes (e.g. smelting) can change the radioactive behaviour of a radioactive substance.

HT An atom has a nucleus made of protons and neutrons. Every atom of a particular **element** always has the same number of protons (if it contained a different number of protons it would be a different element). For example...

Hydrogen atoms have 1 proton
Helium atoms have 2 protons
Oxygen atoms have 8 protons

However, some atoms of the same element can have different numbers of neutrons – these are called **isotopes**. For example, there are three isotopes of oxygen:

Oxygen-16   Oxygen-17   Oxygen-18
has 8 neutrons   has 9 neutrons   has 10 neutrons.

All 3 of these isotopes have 8 protons.

Ionising Radiation

There are three types of radiation that can be given out by radioactive materials. These radiations are **alpha**, **beta** and **gamma**.

Different radioactive materials will give out any one, or a combination, of these radiations.

An easy way to tell which type of radiation you are dealing with is to test its penetrating power.

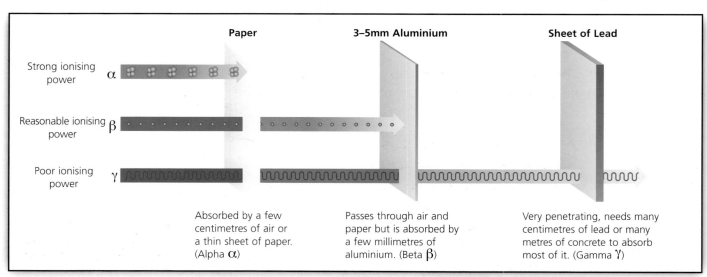

	Paper	3–5mm Aluminium	Sheet of Lead
Strong ionising power	α		
Reasonable ionising power	β		
Poor ionising power	γ		

Absorbed by a few centimetres of air or a thin sheet of paper. (Alpha α)

Passes through air and paper but is absorbed by a few millimetres of aluminium. (Beta β)

Very penetrating, needs many centimetres of lead or many metres of concrete to absorb most of it. (Gamma γ)

Radioactive Materials

Radioactive Decay

The emission of ionising radiation occurs because the nucleus of an unstable atom is decaying. The type of decay depends on why the nucleus is unstable; the process of decay helps make the atom become more stable. During decay the number of protons in the atom may change. If this happens the element changes from one type to another.

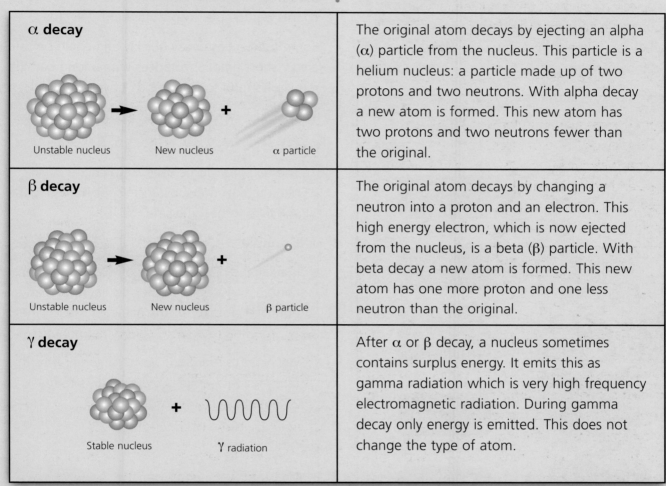

α decay	The original atom decays by ejecting an alpha (α) particle from the nucleus. This particle is a helium nucleus: a particle made up of two protons and two neutrons. With alpha decay a new atom is formed. This new atom has two protons and two neutrons fewer than the original.
Unstable nucleus → New nucleus + α particle	
β decay	The original atom decays by changing a neutron into a proton and an electron. This high energy electron, which is now ejected from the nucleus, is a beta (β) particle. With beta decay a new atom is formed. This new atom has one more proton and one less neutron than the original.
Unstable nucleus → New nucleus + β particle	
γ decay	After α or β decay, a nucleus sometimes contains surplus energy. It emits this as gamma radiation which is very high frequency electromagnetic radiation. During gamma decay only energy is emitted. This does not change the type of atom.
Stable nucleus + γ radiation	

Background Radiation

Radioactive elements are found naturally in the environment. The radiation produced by these sources contributes to the overall background radiation.

There is nothing we can do to prevent ourselves from being **irradiated** and **contaminated** by background radiation, but the level of background radiation in most places is so low that it is nothing to worry about. There is, however, a correlation between certain cancers and living in particular areas, especially among people who have lived in granite buildings for many years.

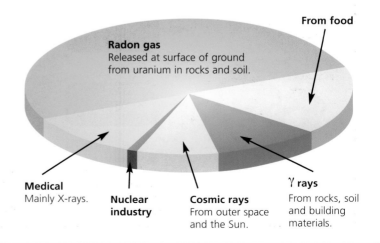

From food

Radon gas
Released at surface of ground from uranium in rocks and soil.

Medical
Mainly X-rays.

Nuclear industry

Cosmic rays
From outer space and the Sun.

γ rays
From rocks, soil and building materials.

Radioactive Materials

Half-life

The activity of a substance is a measure of the amount of radiation given out per second.

When a radioactive atom decays it becomes less radioactive and its activity drops. The **half-life** of a substance is the time it takes for the radioactivity of the substance to halve. The half-life of a radioactive material can range from a few seconds to thousands of years.

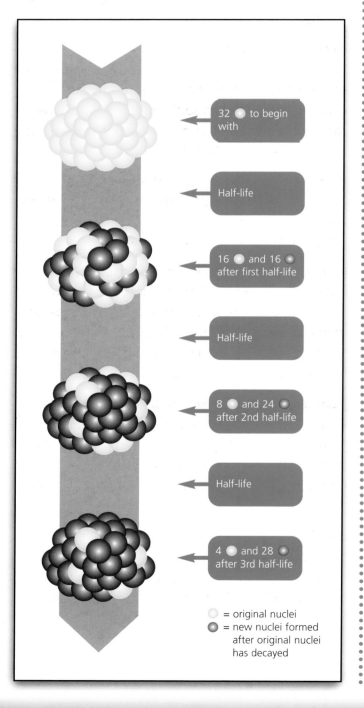

32 ● to begin with

Half-life

16 ● and 16 ● after first half-life

Half-life

8 ● and 24 ● after 2nd half-life

Half-life

4 ● and 28 ● after 3rd half-life

○ = original nuclei
● = new nuclei formed after original nuclei has decayed

Half-life and Safety

All radioactive substances become less radioactive as time passes. A substance would be considered safe once its activity had dropped to the same level emitted as background radiation, which is a dose of around 2 milli sievert per year (see p.81) or 25 counts per minute with a standard detector.

Some substances decay quickly and could be safe in a very short time. Substances with a long half-life remain harmful for thousands of years.

HT Half-life Calculations

The half-life can be used to calculate how old a radioactive substance is, or how long it will take to become safe.

Example

If a sample has an activity of 800 counts per minute and a half-life of 2 hours, how many hours will it take for the activity to reach the background rate of 25 counts per minute?

We need to work out how many half-lives it takes for the sample of 800 counts to reach 25 counts.

1. $\frac{800}{2} = 400$

2. $\frac{400}{2} = 200$

3. $\frac{200}{2} = 100$

4. $\frac{100}{2} = 50$

5. $\frac{50}{2} = 25$

It takes 5 half-lives to reach a count of 25, and each half-life takes 2 hours, so it takes…

5 x 2 hours = 10 hours.

Dangers of Radiation

Ionising radiation can break molecules into ions (see p.51) which can be harmful for living cells (see p.52).

New scientific advances often create an element of risk. The transportation and application of radioactive substances is carefully controlled by government rules and regulations to minimise the risk to the general public. However, people working in the nuclear industry, medical physics (X-rays, etc.), and many other areas often have to work with radioactive materials. They can become irradiated or contaminated by the materials which could lead to serious health problems or even death. Therefore, the exposure that these people are subjected to needs to be carefully monitored.

The different types of radiation carry different risks:

- Alpha is the most dangerous if the source is inside the body; all the radiation will be absorbed by cells in the body.
- Beta is the most dangerous if the source is outside the body, because unlike alpha it can penetrate the outer layer of skin and damage the internal organs.
- Gamma can cause harm if it is absorbed by the cells in the body, but it is weakly ionising and can pass straight through the body causing no damage at all.

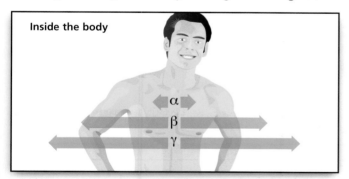

Inside the body

α
β
γ

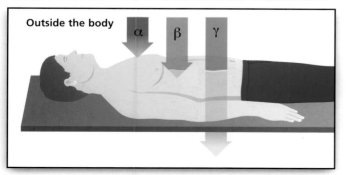

Outside the body

α β γ

The sievert is a measure of a radiation dose's potential to do harm to a person. It is based on both the type and the amount of radiation absorbed. A 5 sievert dose is a 5 sievert dose regardless of the type of radiation absorbed. This makes the sievert a very useful unit for radiation safety measures.

Uses of Radiation

Although using ionising radiation can be dangerous, there are many beneficial uses.

Cancer Treatment

High-energy gamma rays can be used to destroy cancer cells, however, ionising radiation can damage living cells too so the radiation has to be carefully targeted from different angles to minimise the damage to healthy cells.

Radioactive iodine can be used to target thyroid cancer. Iodine is needed by the thyroid, so it collects naturally in the thyroid where it gives out beta radiation and destroys the cancer cells.

In both of these examples there is a danger of damage to healthy cells so the doctors need to carefully weigh the risks against the benefits before going ahead with the procedure. When deciding on the dose of radiation to use, the **ALARA** principle would be applied (see p.56).

Sterilising Surgical Instruments

Bacteria are living cells so are also susceptible to damage from ionising radiation. Gamma radiation is used to kill the bacteria on sealed surgical instruments which then remain sterile until they are ready to be used.

Sterilising Food

Irradiating food kills any bacteria which would cause the food to go off. Radiation treatment is only allowed on a few foods in the UK and these have to carry a label stating that they have been treated with radiation.

Radioactive Materials

Electricity

Electricity is called a **secondary energy source** because it is generated from another energy source e.g. coal, nuclear, wind, etc.

As part of the generation process some energy is always lost to the surroundings. This makes electricity less efficient than when using the primary resource directly.

However, the convenience of electricity makes it very useful. It can be easily transmitted over long distances, and used in a variety of ways.

Generating Electricity

To generate electricity, fuel (either fossil fuel or nuclear) is burned to produce heat.

The heat is used to boil water which produces steam, and the steam is then used to drive the turbines which power the generators.

The electricity produced in the generators is sent to a transformer and then to the national grid from where we can access it in our homes.

In a **fossil fuel** power station the fuel is burned to release the chemical energy it contains as heat. As they are burning carbon fuels, the power stations also produce carbon dioxide, a greenhouse gas (see p.53).

In a **nuclear** power station the energy is released due to changes in the nucleus of radioactive substances. Nuclear power stations do not produce carbon dioxide but they do produce **radioactive waste**. This nuclear waste is categorised into three types:

- **High-level waste** (HLW) – very radioactive waste that has to be stored carefully. Fortunately, only small amounts are produced and it does not last long, so it is put into short-term storage.
- **Intermediate-level waste** (ILW) – not as radioactive as HLW but it does remain radioactive for thousands of years. The amount produced is increasing; deciding how to store it safely and permanently is a problem. At the moment most ILW is mixed with concrete and stored in big containers, but this is not a permanent solution.
- **Low-level waste** (LLW) – only slightly radioactive waste that is sealed and placed in landfills.

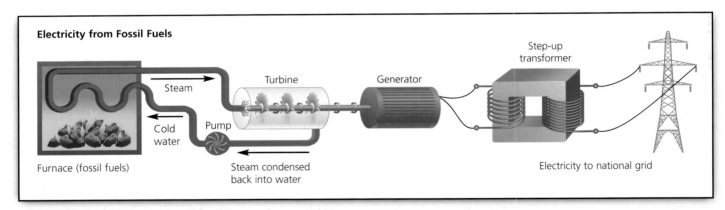

Electricity from Fossil Fuels

Furnace (fossil fuels) · Steam · Cold water · Pump · Steam condensed back into water · Turbine · Generator · Step-up transformer · Electricity to national grid

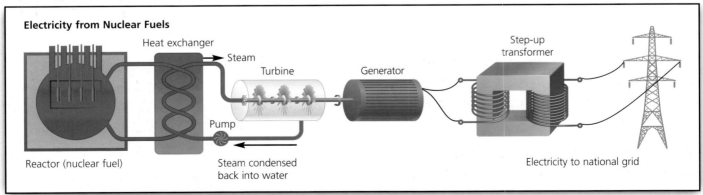

Electricity from Nuclear Fuels

Reactor (nuclear fuel) · Heat exchanger · Steam · Pump · Steam condensed back into water · Turbine · Generator · Step-up transformer · Electricity to national grid

Losing Energy

Energy is lost at every stage of the process of electricity generation. **Sankey diagrams** can by used to show the generation and distribution of electricity, including the efficiency of energy transfers.

The diagram below shows that from the energy put into the power station almost half is lost to the surroundings (mostly as heat) before the electricity even reaches the home.

Further energy is lost during energy transfers in the home when the electricity is used.

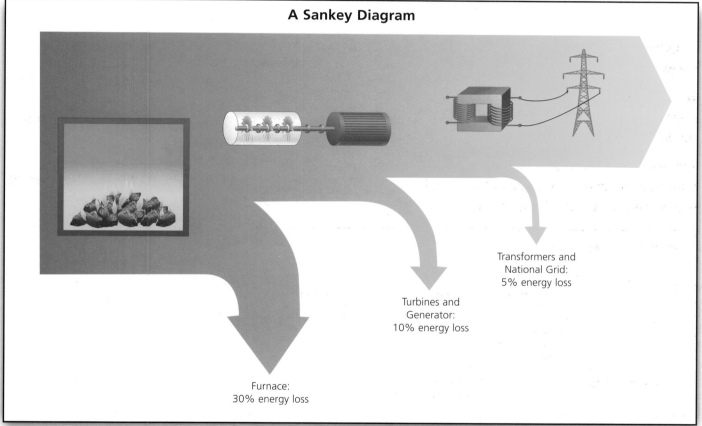

A Sankey Diagram

Transformers and
National Grid:
5% energy loss

Turbines and
Generator:
10% energy loss

Furnace:
30% energy loss

Renewable Energy

Because conventional energy supplies are running out and both nuclear and fossil fuels cause environmental damage, alternative energy sources are becoming more important.

You need to be able to describe two ways of using renewable energy sources to generate electricity.

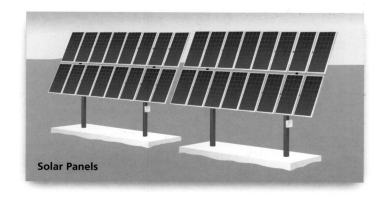

Solar Panels

Radioactive Materials

Renewable Energy (continued)

Wind Turbines

The force of the wind turns the blades of the wind turbine; this provides power to a generator which produces electricity. The amount of electricity produced by wind turbines is small and you would need hundreds of wind turbines to replace one conventional power station. However, once built they provide free energy as long as the wind is blowing.

Hydroelectric Dam

Water stored in the reservoir flows down pipes and turns the turbines which powers the generators and produces electricity. Large areas of land may need to be flooded to build hydroelectric stations. However, once they have been built they provide large amounts of reliable, fairly cheap energy.

Comparing Benefits

When comparing energy sources for generating electricity, you will be given information and will need to assess which source is the most favourable, based on the following factors: efficiency, cost and environmental damage.

> **HT** Power output and lifetime (how long it lasts for) can also be assessed when comparing energy sources.

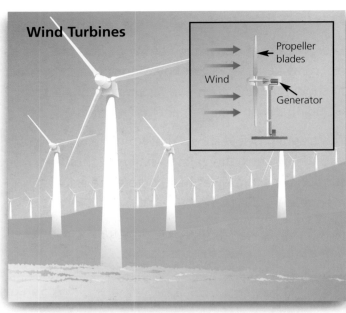

Wind Turbines

Propeller blades

Wind

Generator

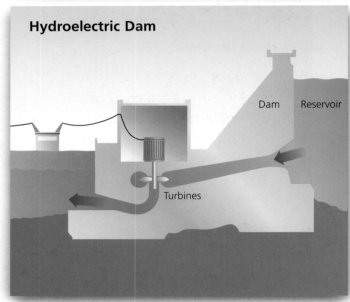

Hydroelectric Dam

Dam   Reservoir

Turbines

Examples

Energy Source	Set Up Cost	Power Output	Efficiency	Environmental Damage
Nuclear	Very high	**HT** High	Good	• Nuclear waste
Coal	High	**HT** High	Good	• Mining (construction and any waste) • Acid rain • Greenhouse gases • Transport of fuel
Wind	Low	**HT** Low	Variable daily	• Need lots • Visual pollution
Hydroelectric	High	**HT** High	Needs rain	• Changes ecosystem through flooding

Nuclear Fission

In a chemical reaction it is the electrons that bring about the change. The elements involved remain the same but join up in different ways.

A fission reaction takes place in the nucleus of the atom and different elements are formed. A neutron (see p.78) is absorbed by a large and unstable **uranium** nucleus. This splits the nucleus into two, roughly equal-sized, smaller nuclei and releases energy and more neutrons. A fission reaction releases far more energy than even the most **exothermic** chemical reactions. Once fission has taken place the neutrons released can be absorbed by other nuclei and further fission reactions can take place. This is called a **chain reaction.**

A chain reaction occurs when there is enough fissile material to prevent too many neutrons escaping without being absorbed. This is called critical mass and ensures every reaction triggers at least one further reaction (see opposite).

The Nuclear Reactor

Nuclear power stations use fission reactions to generate the heat needed to boil water into steam. The reactor controls the **chain reaction** so that the energy is released at a steady rate.

Fission occurs in the **fuel rods** and causes them to become very hot.

The **coolant** is a liquid that is pumped through the reactor. The coolant heats up and is then used in the heat exchanger to turn water into steam.

Control rods, made of boron, absorb neutrons preventing the chain reaction getting out of control. Moving the control rods in and out of the reactor core changes the amount of fission which takes place.

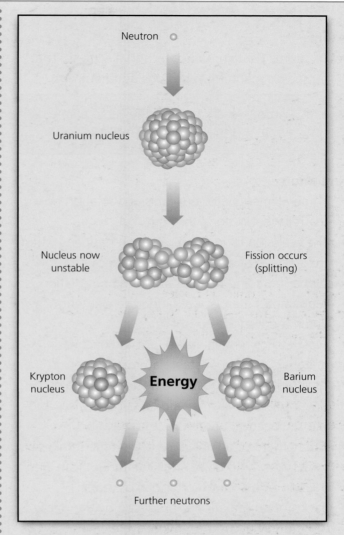

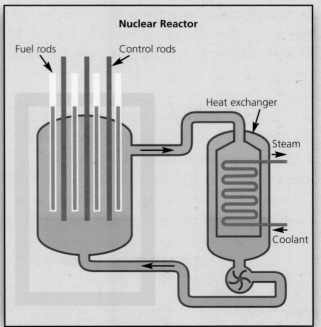

Radioactive Materials – Summary

Science Explanations

Atoms

- All atoms contain a nucleus and electrons. The nucleus is made from protons and neutrons.

> **HT** • An isotope is an atom of the same element but with a different number of neutrons.

Radiation

- Some elements give out ionising radiation no matter what is done to them.
- The emission of ionising radiation happens when the nucleus of an unstable atom decays.
- Alpha, beta and gamma are ionising radiation.
- Alpha and beta decay change the element, gamma emissions do not.
- Most atoms remain stable, but radioactive materials contain unstable atoms.
- As a radioactive substance decays it contains fewer unstable atoms, and so becomes less and less radioactive, and emits less radiation.
- The half-life of a substance is the time it takes for its activity to halve. This can range from a fraction of a second to billions of years.
- Background radiation is produced by the decay of naturally occurring radioactive elements, medical equipment and the nuclear industry.
- We are irradiated and contaminated all the time by background radiation, but it is at a very low level.
- Ionising radiation can damage or destroy cells.
- People working with radioactive materials need to have their exposure levels regularly checked.
- The different types of radiation carry different risks for people, depending on whether the source is inside or outside the body.
- The sievert is a measure of the radiation dose as a potential to do harm to a person, based on both the type and amount of radiation received.
- Ionising radiation can destroy cancer cells and sterilise food and surgical equipment.

Nuclear Power

- In a nuclear power station the energy is released because of changes in the nucleus. Nuclear power stations produce radioactive waste.

> **HT** • Nuclear fission takes place in the nucleus of the atom. It releases far more energy than chemical reactions.
> • A nuclear reactor uses a controlled chain reaction to generate heat for producing electricity.

Electricity

- Electricity is a secondary energy source. A primary energy source is needed to generate it.
- It can be easily transferred and used to produce different energies as required: kinetic, light, sound, heat.
- In most power stations a fuel is used to boil water. This produces steam, which turns a turbine, which rotates a generator.

Energy Sources

- We often need a source of energy to change things in some way or make things happen.
- Fuels like coal, oil, natural gas and wood are valuable and concentrated sources of energy.
- Fossil fuels are non-renewable energy sources.
- Renewable energy sources include wind, waves, tides, solar energy, dammed rainwater, and wood.
- Radioactive elements, such as uranium, release energy as they decay. This can produce geothermal energy.

Ideas about Science

Risk, Science and Technology

- New technologies and processes based on scientific advances often introduce new risks.
- Any activity contains a certain risk of accident/harm.

> **HT** • The ALARA principle suggests a balance between risk and benefit.

- In many areas of scientific work, officials, regulations and laws control how science is used.

The Exam Paper

One of the aims of OCR GCSE Science A is to develop your knowledge and understanding of key scientific explanations and ideas, so that you can evaluate information about important science-based issues and make informed personal decisions where necessary.

In addition to your coursework (a case study and practical data analysis), which is assessed by your teacher, you will have to sit four exams.

The first three papers will focus on the scientific explanations and ideas covered in Units 1, 2 and 3 respectively (covered on pages 6-86 of this revision guide).

The fourth paper will test your understanding of ideas in context. The questions will be based on current science-based issues (which you may well be aware of from coverage in the media). To answer them you will have to recall relevant scientific facts and draw upon your knowledge of how science works, i.e. the practices and procedures involved in collecting scientific evidence, and its impact on society.

This section of the revision guide looks at the Ideas in Context exam paper in more detail so you will know exactly what to expect.

It clarifies how many marks the paper represents and looks at the type of questions that may come up, the format they are likely to take, and what skills you will need to use to answer them.

Exam Details

Title: OCR Science A Unit 4 – Ideas
in Context

Duration: 45 minutes

Total Mark: 40

Weighting: 16.7% (of total mark for course)

The paper will consist of three structured questions (i.e. questions with several parts) and you must answer all of them.

You will sit either the foundation paper or the higher paper. This will be decided with your teacher before the build up to exams.

Ideas in Context

Question Format

Each of the three questions will be based on a different topic from the specification. Each year, the topics featured in the exam are chosen at random. However, they are always taken from the three separate subject areas, so there will be one biology question, one chemistry question and one physics question.

Do not worry, you will not be asked questions relating to any topics other than those on the specification.

At the start of each question you will be presented with some facts and information about a science-based issue connected to the chosen topic. This could be written information, data (i.e. tables and graphs), or a combination of both.

This information will be sent to your school before the exam. Your teachers will give you the information in a science lesson a set number of days before the exam. You will be able to read through the text in class and look up any technical terms or phrases that you do not understand. You are not expected to do further research but you should revise any of the relevant scientific explanations or ideas.

You will not be able to take the original articles or any notes into the exam.

You will then be presented with a series of questions relating to that issue. They can take a variety of formats, from multiple choice and matching questions to data analysis and questions that require a written response.

The questions will be designed to test…
- your understanding of the information
- your understanding of related scientific explanations
- your understanding of the practices and procedures used in scientific investigations
- your ability to identify the benefits and drawbacks of the science and technology involved
- your ability to identify the different arguments surrounding the issue (i.e. for and against)
- your ability to evaluate the impact of the technology involved on the environment and society.

The next few pages include an exam-style question, with model answers and handy hints on how to approach the different parts of the question.

Sample Question

Question 1

This magazine article is about a high-profile drug trial that occurred in March 2006.

Drug Trial Horror for Volunteers

In March 2006, six healthy volunteers ended up fighting for their lives in hospital intensive care after participating in trials of a new drug designed to treat leukaemia.

The trial involved eight paid volunteers. The six men who received the drug fell ill suddenly after being administered the injection, suffering multiple organ failure, while the two remaining volunteers who received a placebo did not.

The industry watchdog, the Medicines and Healthcare Products Regulatory Agency (MHRA), stopped the drug trial and alerted other European countries of the problem immediately so that no further trials would be carried out.

The men were given the drug, called TGN1412, at an independent medical research unit operated by a US drug research company as part of a phase one trial.

Phase one trials follow rigorous animal testing. The research company claims that the results of their initial laboratory studies and animal testing gave no hint of the terrible side effects, so the organ failure suffered by the volunteers was completely unexpected.

Such an adverse reaction to a drug is very rare in first-time tests on humans. There will usually be some indication of a problem at the animal testing stage and, as a result, the drug will not be authorised for trials involving humans.

There are four key phases to clinical drug trials involving human volunteers:

Phase One: these trials can only be carried out if animal testing indicates the drug is safe and effective. They are carried out on a small number of volunteers to test the safety of the drug and to determine an appropriate dosage.

Phase Two: the aim of these trials is to provide evidence that the drug is efficient. If the drug is expected to have a dramatic effect, the numbers may be small. However, in most cases, a large sample group is needed to produce reliable data.

Phase Three: these trials compare the efficiency and side effects of the new drug with other drugs, treatments and placebos. These are usually large trials, using groups of volunteers at lots of different centres throughout the UK or Europe, and can continue for several years. If the drug is successful at this phase, a licence may be issued.

Phase Four: these are long-term studies, normally carried out by the medical and pharmaceuticals industry, which can last for ten years or more. They involve collating detailed information, looking at the long-term effects and the overall impact of the drug on patients, the disease and society.

The question information above is based on the content in Module B2: Keeping Healthy. It focuses specifically on the methods used for testing new drugs. Make sure you read all the information carefully before you even attempt to answer the questions.

The information in this question is taken from a magazine article. It is important to remember that articles in the media may be biased, i.e. they do not always give a balanced account. Other sources that might contain bias include marketing information, advertising, letters etc.

Ideas in Context

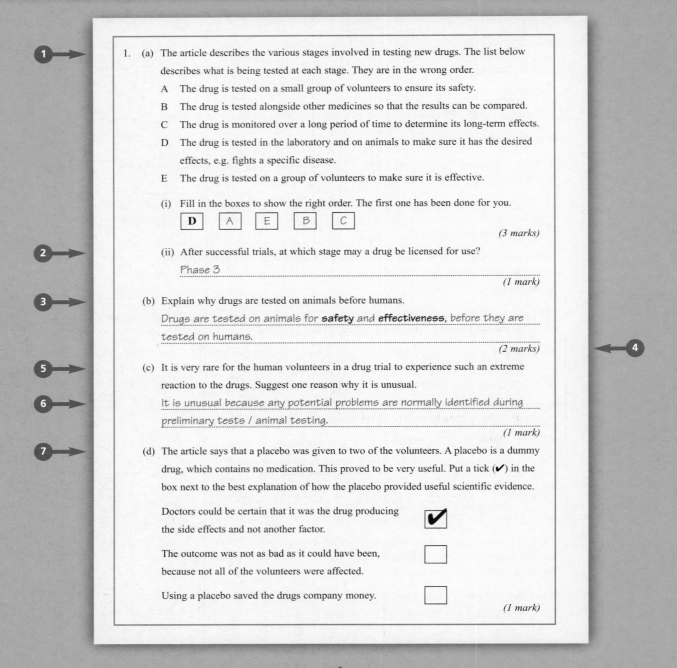

1. (a) The article describes the various stages involved in testing new drugs. The list below describes what is being tested at each stage. They are in the wrong order.

A   The drug is tested on a small group of volunteers to ensure its safety.

B   The drug is tested alongside other medicines so that the results can be compared.

C   The drug is monitored over a long period of time to determine its long-term effects.

D   The drug is tested in the laboratory and on animals to make sure it has the desired effects, e.g. fights a specific disease.

E   The drug is tested on a group of volunteers to make sure it is effective.

(i)   Fill in the boxes to show the right order. The first one has been done for you.

| **D** | A | E | B | C |

(3 marks)

(ii)   After successful trials, at which stage may a drug be licensed for use?

Phase 3

(1 mark)

(b)   Explain why drugs are tested on animals before humans.

Drugs are tested on animals for **safety** and **effectiveness**, before they are tested on humans.

(2 marks)

(c)   It is very rare for the human volunteers in a drug trial to experience such an extreme reaction to the drugs. Suggest one reason why it is unusual.

It is unusual because any potential problems are normally identified during preliminary tests / animal testing.

(1 mark)

(d)   The article says that a placebo was given to two of the volunteers. A placebo is a dummy drug, which contains no medication. This proved to be very useful. Put a tick (✔) in the box next to the best explanation of how the placebo provided useful scientific evidence.

Doctors could be certain that it was the drug producing the side effects and not another factor.   ✔

The outcome was not as bad as it could have been, because not all of the volunteers were affected.   ☐

Using a placebo saved the drugs company money.   ☐

(1 mark)

---

1 To answer this question you need to arrange the descriptions into the correct order. It is testing your general understanding of the information – you can answer it correctly by referring back to the text. This type of question can look easy, but make sure you take your time and read each description carefully to avoid making silly mistakes.

2 This part of the question is testing how carefully you read the information. The answer is in the text, but you might have missed it if you were skim reading.

3 To answer this question you need to recall what you learnt about how drugs are tested in Module B2. However, even if you cannot remember the exact reasons, you should be able to gain at least one mark by using your common sense.

4 Look at the marks for each question (given on the right-hand side of the question paper) – they will give you a clue as to how much information you need to give. This question is worth two marks: one for mentioning safety and one for mentioning effectiveness.

5 Again, this question is testing your understanding of the information given and the procedures used to test new drugs. By referring back to the text, you should find the answer in paragraph 6.

6 Your answer does not have to be word perfect, as long as you mention the tests that are carried out before human trials are allowed to take place.

7 You do not need to know what a placebo is beforehand because it is explained in the question and you can work out the correct answer by reading the information you are given. In the text you are told that the volunteers who took the placebo did not experience the same side effects as those who took the drug. So, assuming that all other factors were the same, this shows that the drug must have been responsible. Placebos are used in trials in the same way that control experiments are used in the laboratory.

This is another type of multiple choice question. If all else fails, you should be able to eliminate the two wrong answers because they do not relate to how scientific evidence is obtained.

(e) The methods used for preliminary drug testing are controversial. Evaluate one method, describing at least two different views that may be held.

✏ One mark is for a clear, ordered answer.

New drugs can be tested on human cells grown in the laboratory. This method shows whether the drugs are damaging to human cells, **although** it does not show how they will affect the human body as a whole. In this method of testing no animals or people are harmed. **On the other hand**, some people believe that growing human cells in this way is unnatural and wrong.

or

New drugs can be tested on animals. This method shows whether the drugs can work effectively within an organism, **however**, animals might react differently from humans. This method shows if the drugs are safe for an organism, **but** animals can suffer pain and die as a result of the tests.

(3 + 1 marks)

(f) In this trial, the drug was tested on healthy volunteers. However, phase two, three and four trials, commonly use volunteers with the illness that the drug is intended to treat.

(i) What is being tested in phase one trials? Put a ring around the correct answer.

(Safety)   Efficiency   Long-term effects

(1 mark)

ii) What is being tested in phase two trials? Put a ring around the correct answer.

Safety   (Efficiency)   Long-term effects

(1 mark)

g) Why is it important for phase two trials to include patients with the illness?

It is only possible to test a drug's efficiency at treating a disease if it is used on people with the disease.

(1 mark)

15

---

8 Read the question carefully – it is referring to preliminary drug tests, not clinical trials. So, you could have referred to one of two methods of drug testing to answer this question.

9 Using connectives to join your sentences together makes your answer easier to read and helps to distinguish between two separate points. In the model answers above, the connectives are written in bold.

10 This question is worth three marks, and the pencil symbol ✏ means that an extra mark is available for a clear, ordered answer. To gain full marks you need to say what method of testing you are referring to (1 mark), and clearly state two different views that may be held (1 mark each). To earn the extra mark, make sure you write in clear sentences and order them in a logical way. For example, describe one method of testing, give one advantage of that method, and then give one disadvantage of that method. Finally, make sure your spelling, punctuation and grammar are all correct.

11 These are multiple choice questions. You can answer both these questions correctly by referring back to the descriptions of the different phases in the text. With multiple choice questions like these, even if you do not know it immediately, you can sometimes arrive at the correct answer by eliminating the wrong answers one at a time.

12 This question is a bit harder than the rest, because the answer is not in the text. But do not be put off – it just requires a bit of careful thinking and common sense.

13 Remember, you answer does not have to match the one on the mark scheme word for word, as long as you have identified the fact that the purpose of a drug is to treat a specific disease, so it can only be tested for efficiency and effectiveness on volunteers with that disease.

Ideas in Context

Exam and Revision Tips

- Try to watch the news and read newspapers and publications like *New Scientist, BBC Focus* and *Flipside* whenever you can – this will alert you to any topical science-based issues that might come up on the exam paper. You should be able to find these in your school library or resource centre. You can also find websites for these publications with up-to-date information.
- Before the exam, you need to revise all the scientific ideas and explanations on the specification (covered on pages 6–86 of this revision guide).
- It may sound obvious, but make sure you read the information carefully before attempting to answer any of the questions. Underline key words and try breaking up the sentences. This will help you to focus on the content of the question.
- The answers to many of the questions will be in the information, so keep referring back to it.

- The total marks available for each question are shown in the right-hand margin. The marks allocated and the space provided should give you a clue as to the length of answer required and how much information you need to give. For example, if a written question is worth two marks, the examiner is likely to be looking for two key points in your answer.
- If you are asked to make a calculation, always show your working. Marks are often given if you use the correct method, even if the answer is incorrect.
- If you are giving a measurement, make sure you remember to include the units and use the correct abbreviation.
- For some questions an extra mark may be awarded for the quality of written communication of your answer. If this is the case, a pencil icon will be shown (✐) and it will say so clearly on the paper. This means you should…
  - write in clear sentences
  - order your sentences in a logical way
  - use correct spelling, punctuation and grammar
  - use the correct scientific words.

Glossary

Activity – (Physics) the amount of radioactive decay per second

Adaptation – the gradual change of a particular organism over generations to become better suited to its environment

Atom – smallest part of an element that displays the chemical properties of the element

Biodiversity – the variety amongst living organisms and ecosystems in which they live

Cell – fundamental unit of a living organism

Chromosome – a coil of DNA made up of genes, found in the nucleus of plant / animal cells

Clones – individuals that are genetically identical to the parent

Combustion – chemical reaction which occurs when fuels burn, releasing heat

Compound – a substance consisting of two or more elements chemically combined together

Contamination – radioactive material that can get into, or onto, a person

Decompose – to break down

Diabetes – a disease caused by the pancreas not producing and releasing (enough) insulin

Deoxyribonucleic acid (DNA) – nucleic acid which contains the genetic information carried by every cell in an organism

Effector – the part of the body, e.g. a muscle or a gland, which produces a response to a stimulus

Element – a substance that consists of one type of atom

Embryo – a ball of cells which will develop into a human / animal baby

Epidemiology – the study of a disease in the population

Eutrophication – the enrichment of water by nutrients, especially compounds of nitrogen and / or phosphorus, producing low-oxygenated water and a greater concentration of plant life over animal life

Evolve – to change naturally over a period of time

Extinct – a species that has died out

Fertilisation – the fusion of the male nucleus with the female nucleus

Fetus – an unborn animal / human baby

Finite – limited

Food chain – the feeding relationship between organisms in an ecosystem

Fossil fuels – fuels formed in the ground, over millions of years, from the remains of dead plants and animals

Fuel – a substance that releases heat or energy when combined with oxygen

Galaxy – a huge system of stars, dust and gas held together by gravity

Gene – part of a chromosome, composed of DNA

Genetic testing – testing individuals to determine if they have any genetic diseases

Geohazard – any natural hazard associated with the Earth, e.g. earthquakes and volcanoes

Global warming – an increase in average global temperatures due to an increase in levels of greenhouse gases

Gravity – a force of attraction between masses

Greenhouse gases – gases in the Earth's atmosphere that stop radiation from leaving the Earth's surface

Half-life – the time taken for half the atoms in radioactive material to decay

Hormone – a regulatory substance which stimulates cells or tissues into action

Hydrocarbon – a compound containing only hydrogen and carbon atoms

Intensive farming – a method of farming which seeks to maximise production with the use of chemical fertilisers, herbicides and pesticides

Ions – a charged particle formed when an atom gains or loses electrons

Isotope – atoms of the same element but with a different number of neutrons

IVF – a technique in which egg cells are fertilised outside the woman's body

Life Cycle Assessment – an assessment of a product from manufacture to disposal

Mutation – a change in the genetic material of a cell

Natural selection – a natural process resulting in the evolution of organisms best adapted to the environment

Glossary

Neurone – specialised cell which transmits electrical messages or nerve impulses

Nitrogen cycle – the circulation of nitrogen; nitrates from the soil are absorbed by plants which are eaten by animals that die and decay, returning the nitrogen back to the soil.

Non-biodegradable – a substance that does not decompose naturally

Non-renewable energy – energy sources that cannot be replaced within a lifetime

Nuclear fission – the splitting of atomic nuclei

Nuclear fusion – the joining of atomic nuclei

Obesity – the condition of being very overweight

Organic farming – farming without the use of artificial fertilisers or pesticides and with an emphasis on quality rather than quantity

Pesticide – a substance used for destroying insects or other pests

Photons – packets of energy

Photosynthesis – the chemical process used by plants where water combines with carbon dioxide to produce glucose using light energy

Pollutants – chemicals that can harm the environment and health

Polymer – a giant long-chain hydrocarbon

Recycling – the re-use of materials that would otherwise be considered waste

Renewable energy – energy sources that can be replaced

Selective breeding – when animals are deliberately mated to produce offspring with desirable characteristics

Solar system – the collection of nine planets, and their moons, in orbit around the Sun.

Species – a group of organisms that can breed freely with each other to produce fertile offspring

Subduction – when an oceanic tectonic plate is forced under a continental plate

Sustainable development – a policy to meet the needs of the present generation without compromising the ability of future generations to meet their own needs

Tectonic plates – huge sections of the Earth's crust which move relative to one another

Universe – a collection of galaxies

Vaccine – a liquid preparation used to make the body produce antibodies in order to provide protection against disease

Variation – differences between individuals of the same species

Index

Notes